THE FREUDIAN MOMENT

First published in 2007 by
Karnac Books Ltd
118 Finchley Road, London NW3 5HT

Reprinted 2008

British Library Cataloguing in Publication Data

A C.I.P. for this book is available from the British Library

ISBN 978 1 85575 575 8

Edited, designed and produced by The Studio Publishing Services Ltd
www.studiopublishingservicesuk.co.uk
e-mail: studio@publishingservices.co.uk

10 9 8 7 6 5 4 3 2 1

www.karnacbooks.com

CONTENTS

ACKNOWLEDGEMENTS

Thanks to Michael Eigen, Editor of *Psychoanalytic Review*, and the *National Psychological Association for Psychoanalysis* for permission to publish "Perceptive identification", which was published in *Psychoanalytic Review*, 93(5), October, 2006, pp. 713–717.

Thanks to Dr André Green and PUF for permission to reprint "De l'interprétation du transfert comme résistance à l'association libre", in Green et al. (2006) *Les Voies Nouvelles de la Therapeutique Psychoanalytique*, Paris.

Christopher Bollas is a member of the British Psychoanalytical Society, the Los Angeles Institute and Society for Psychoanalytic Studies, and Honorary Member of the Institute for Psychoanalytic Training and Research. He is a member of ESGUT, the European Study Group of Unconscious Thought.

Vincenzo Bonaminio is a training and supervising analyst of the Italian Psychoanalytic Society and a member of the faculty of the Institute of Child Neuropsychiatry of the University of Rome ("La Sapienza"). He has a private practice in Rome.

Introduction

The interviews, talks, and essays that form this book took place in 2006. They illuminate Bollas's most recent considerations on unconscious thinking and, in particular, his view that we need to rethink unconscious articulation.

At the invitation of the European Psychoanalytic Federation (EPF) I interviewed Christopher Bollas at the Athens Conference in April of 2006. As the text needed to be translated for the Conference, we conducted the interview by e-mail. It drew so much interest from those attending that we agreed to a follow-up, which constitutes the second chapter of this book.

"What is theory?" is a talk given by Bollas at the International Federation of Psychoanalytic Education's (IFPE) Annual Conference in Pasadena, California in November of 2006. There, Bollas received the Hans Loewald Award for outstanding contributions to psychoanalysis, and his talk was delivered as part of that celebration. Along with his essay "Perceptive identification", it address the question not only of how theory constitutes a form of unconscious perception, but also how an object of perception has objective qualities open for unconscious apprehension. In "On transference interpretation as a resistance to free association", one finds variations on the themes in the earlier chapters, now organized to provide a devastating critique of an excess in psychoanalytical technique—the here and now transference interpretation. The essay was selected by the German Psychoanalytical Association (DPV and DPG) to be the object of debate at its Annual Conference in March of 2007.

This collection reveals something of the depth, range, and creative insight of Bollas's thinking, presented here very much as "work in progress".

I first met Christopher Bollas in 1977. By invitation of Andreas Giannakoulas, who, together with Adriano Giannotti founded a Training Programme in Child and Adolescent Psychoanalytic Psychotherapy inside the University of Rome that has been running since 1976, a number of outstanding psychoanalysts visited the Institute of Child Neuropsychiatry to contribute their expertise to the clinical training of the students. Among them, Paula Heimann, Frances Tustin, Marion Milner, Adam Limentani, and Christopher Bollas himself have left the most durable traces of their influence in what has become *our clinical tradition* over the years.

Christopher Bollas was at the time a young and brilliant psychoanalyst (many of us were then even younger students). He deeply impressed us with his outstanding and seminal paper on the *trans - formational object*. He presented a paper before a deeply engaged audience; it became soon after a sort of "foundational" contribution, in so far as it helped us to conceive and understand, in a different, more complex dynamic, the mutual *unconscious* relationship between mother and child (an issue that was at stake for us as child analysts *in fieri*), and how the object affects and influences that "thing called self". As he put it years later in *Cracking Up*, "even as an unconscious subject I am still shaped by another's effect on me. My self is given a new form by the *other*" (Bollas, 1995, p. 25).

For me, that paper is still the core, the creative source of the dramatic development that his psychoanalytic contribution achieved in different directions, mainly in unconscious thinking. Both Paula Heimann and Frances Tustin commented to me, in different private contexts when they came to visit the Clinic in the early 1980s, that with his sharp clinical thinking and articulated and creative conceptual understanding, Bollas should be considered a *rising star*, *a promise for psychoanalysis of the future*. The future has come true, the promise has been maintained.

All the essays in his books, from *The Shadow of the Object* through *Cracking Up*, were first presented to an Italian ear and mind. Bollas has long acknowledged that the Italian other is the receptive unconscious to whom he speaks, and our experience is that this may be because Italian psychoanalysis, though informed of the many differing schools of analytical thought, has remained open, with an independent mind.

All of Bollas's books, including his novels, are published in Italian. He has presented his work to all the Italian psychoanalytical societies and has lectured and supervised throughout the country. To us he is part of Italian psychoanalysis, and it is in celebration of this that I say: Grazie Christopher, la tua è stata una stagione di semina così buona in terra italiana che altri, e nuovi, buoni frutti potranno essere colti anche negli anni a venire.

Vincenzo Bonaminio
Rome
March 2007

CHAPTER ONE

Psychic transformations

VB: The theme of our Congress is "Psychic Transformations in the Psychoanalytical Process". In some of your most recent work you argue that the arrival of psychoanalysis *itself* is transformative, in so far as the evolution of the western mind is concerned. Would you care to discuss this?

CB: We can describe the arrival of psychoanalysis as the "Freudian Moment". When Freud invented the psychoanalytical process—the basic method of the free associating analysand and what Adam Phillips so astutely terms the free listening analyst (Phillips, 2002, p. 31)—he fulfilled a search.

As long ago as 2500 BC the Sumerians took their dream life so seriously that they needed and sought interpretation of their dreams. We can think of dreaming as the drive behind a phylogenetic need for dream reporting, the hearing of the dream, and the interpretation of the dream.

Existence was frightening and a single mind was not adequate to think the human condition. Dreaming *itself* must have been a very powerful experience. We may conjecture that dreams frequently overwhelmed the mind because it could not think its contents, even though it was aided by powerful

religious beliefs that acted as containers for anxiety. By reporting the dream to the human other, early man knew that to
survive mental life, it was essential to have the assistance of
the other.

We are familiar with Bion's theory of preconception. For
thousands of years there has been an unconscious preconception of psychoanalysis. We—and by "we" I mean human
beings—have been searching for the Freudian Moment, which
is a realization of this preconception. When Freud *formalized* the
reporting and the reception of the dream he realized this
phylogenetic preconception and a relation we had been seeking for tens of thousands of years was now in place.

In the understandable rush of Freud and the early analysts
to write down their findings there has been some failure on all
of our parts to fully recognize this extraordinary moment.
Indeed, until we think through what we have discovered, we
cannot claim to have conceptualized psychoanalysis. We have
the preconception and intermittent realizations (subject to −K
and therefore lost for a while), but the concept "psychoanalysis" is not secured. The Freudian Moment, however, changed
man forever.

Massacio and other Renaissance painters discovered how
to represent three-dimensional perspective. Visual images of
our world and ourselves would change forever.

Shakespeare dramatized the human mind and human relations in a way that changed the way we think. So has Freud.

VB: It is interesting that you place such an emphasis on psychoanalysis as part of a phylogenetic need, realized in some ways
in order to secure the species.

CB: The Freudian Moment arrived soon after the discovery of
mass armaments that would kill tens of thousands of people.
The horrors of the twentieth century are a warning that we are
on the verge of extinction. Either we understand others and
ourselves, we find a way to think about our conflicts with one
another, to analyse destructive processes, or we cease to exist.
I think psychoanalysis heralded the arrival of the best means
to think about destructive processes. It arrived at the moment
when its implementation might rescue humanity from self-
destruction. So, indeed, I do understand that psychoanalysis,

as a phylogenetic and evolutionary accomplishment, was born of necessity.

VB: You say that you do not think that we have fully conceived of this. By we, do you mean psychoanalysts or do you mean mankind? And if you mean psychoanalysts have not formed a conception of this realization, quite where does that leave us?

CB: The Freudian Moment was immediately obscured by Freud's narcissism, by the grandiose exultations of the early analysts, and by public excitement over its more titillating features such as the theory of infantile sexuality. And although analysts are often realizing psychoanalysis in their clinical work there is no profession "psychoanalysis". Psychoanalysts are still, first, psychiatrists, psychologists, or social workers. Most efforts to create a free standing, independent profession have been opposed. This reflects a failure to conceive psychoanalysis. In addition, while psychoanalytical schools of thought are invaluable means of selecting out particular facts embedded in the realization, and while the writings of Klein, Lacan, Bion, Winnicott, and others are essential to the conception of this realization, the psychoanalytical movements impede thought. Theory is very important, but when it *is used* for purposes of −K, when we use ideas as heralds of political position, then psychoanalytical ideas are reduced to things: to weapons in the psychoanalytic wars.

VB: But aren't such movements, whether in psychoanalysis, literary criticism, or philosophy, an inevitable part of mental life? Isn't this just the clash of ideas?

CB: Intellection and intellectual history—as clash of ideas—are at their best when the clash is part of the life instincts. The critical deconstruction of ideas is crucial to intellectual development. We can think here of Winnicott's concept of the "use of the object" where there must be a ruthless utilization of proposed ideas, and where these ideas are altered through our use of them. For Winnicott, this is an essential feature of ordinary aggression. Similarly, as we use some of Lacan's or Klein's or Kohut's ideas, we *subjectify* them, and, of course, we change them, and some parts of their theory survive, some parts fall into the margins. Such thinking, however, is based on the epistemophilic instinct, which Freud, ambiguously, attached to the sexual instincts (Freud, 1909d, p. 245).

So, when we use ideas as intellectual objects we are going to subjectify them. This is part of the creative clash of ideas.

Too many psychoanalytical movements, however, are allied to the death instinct. Instead of a clash of ideas there is "intellectual genocide" (see Bollas, 1992). One group falsifies another's ideas, and engages in a type of clan warfare. Significant ideas cease to be signifiers and instead become signs, used as things-in-themselves in such warfare. When a signifier becomes a sign it is stripped of its meaning and is no longer of use. When we examine the major movements of psychoanalysis we can see how such movements privilege specific terms—now signs—and in my view such collapsing of the Symbolic order into the Real destroys thinking.

As importantly, if psychoanalysis is to serve the crisis of our times, if we are to be politically effective, then we have to prove the efficacy of insight into our own political realm. To quote Hannah Segal's famous remark, "silence is the real crime". Too often we are silent about corruptions and destructive behaviour amongst analysts and analytical groups.

VB: So what you are saying relates in some respects, then, to the question we are conferring about at this Congress. By your definition the movements retard the psychic transformations possible within the psychoanalytical process.

CB: Yes, that is correct. Psychoanalytical movements usually (although not always) form around a charismatic figure and they become cults that use the words and ideas of that figure to bind their community together. In this way, psychoanalytical movements counteract the creative evolution of psychoanalysis. They are a feature of the death drive because movements retreat into enclaves and do not invest in the ideas of other analytical groups or individual analytical writers.

VB: You claim to be a pluralist, but as you know many—if not most—psychoanalysts would disagree with this proposal. It is argued that the pluralist view seeks, through an ecumenical approach, a kind of politics of inclusion that waters down the core truths of psychoanalysis. From your view one cannot be a Kleinian, or a Kohutian, or a Classical French analyst, because this is contrary to the pluralist ethic. How do you respond to these criticisms, and how does this issue relate to the theme of this Congress?

CB: It depends on how we understand theory. Theories are views. Each theory sees something that the other theories do not see. They are forms of sensation. What we gain from the eyes is different from what we take in from the ears. What we perceive of reality through the olfactory sense is different from what we take in from touch. Theory is a meta-sensual phenomenon. Some theories are better than others, just as it is possible to say that sight is probably more frequently used than smell in the perception of reality. So you can see that for me pluralism is, in its core, a theory of perception, and to say that one must become a Kleinian or a Lacanian, to the exclusion of the other theories, is as absurd as saying that one must become an advocate of the ear, or an eye-guy, or a touch person, or a sniffer.

This issue becomes important when considering psychic transformations in psychoanalysis. If we develop new theories we enhance our perceptual capability. Freud had *at least* three significant models of the mind: (1) the dream work model; (2) the topographic model; (3) the structural model. Sometimes in work with a patient I am aware that I am "seeing" the analysand's material through the topographical model. That allows me to consider certain things in a very clear light, especially repression and the return of the repressed. The dream-work model allows me to "see" how the analysand works lived experience of the day into his or her psychic history that is then condensed into the dream event, which is later deconstructed through the process of free association. In turn, the structural model allows me to "see" how the ego is pressured both by the drives and by the superego. I can "see" compromise formations, for example, better through this theory than I can through any other theory.

These theories reside in the psychoanalyst's preconscious and will be activated by the analyst's need to see certain things at certain times. So if the analyst has been schooled in Freud, Klein, Bion, Winnicott, Lacan, Kohut and others then in my view he has more perceptual capability in his preconscious than an analyst who remains within only one vision.

As I have said, however, I think many analysts would identify themselves with one group but they have in fact become
pluralists without knowing it.

VB: How can one be "all these things" one might ask? Surely you
could not know more about Kohut than, say, a Kohutian. And
a long standing Kleinian would know more about that way of
seeing. Don't you risk trying to be too many perceivers? Do
you not run the risk of shallow transformations based on a
slight grasp of one theory, but at the expense of greater depth?

CB: This is a legitimate question and, indeed, a fair objection.
There is no doubt that I know less of the theoreticians you
mention than those inside these movements in their name. I
do think, however, it is possible to study their writings in
depth and to work with analysts from these schools, so that
one can grasp the basic models they propose and then gain
new sight in one's own work. Indeed, a risk faced by remaining in one of these schools is the scotomatic effect of a canalized vision. They often go too far. Rather than listening to the
analysand with an open mind, they listen out for something
in particular, whether it is the castration complex, the drive
derivative, or the ego position. Such selective listening makes
psychic transformations in analysis possible in so far as the
analytical model is concerned. That is, one can work hard on
gaining more reality orientation and adaptation for the ego,
and one could point to psychic change as a result of this, but
what would not be seen by the clinician, in my view, is that
while something has been transformed within the kingdom of
this selected fact, too much has been lost by virtue of its limi-
tations. The many other transformational possibilities within
analysis will not have been made available.

VB: Can you give an example of a technical approach that is so
worryingly limiting? Presumably you are referring here to a
negative transformation?

CB: There is now a widespread use of what is termed the "here and
now transference interpretation". This is the view that almost
everything the analysand says to the analyst is either a reference to the analyst or an action committed upon the analyst.
This is an example of an extremist approach. It is certainly true
that from time to time the analysand *is* unconsciously referring

to the psychoanalyst, and also it is equally true that often what the analysand says is really, in Austin's sense, an "illocutionary act" (Austin, 1962, pp. 98–164). The insistence that each of these factors is taking place all the time, and that the analyst must interpret this in the transference *throughout the session*, takes the semi-paranoid dimension of the selective fact and turns it into a full-blown idea of reference. I have no doubt that such a listening perspective collapses the analysand's wish to be unconsciously communicative. This may lead the analysand to retreat into an enclave in order to ward off the intense intrusiveness of the analyst. Such a retreat is seen by the analyst as evidence of the invidiously destructive ambition of the analysand's negative transference, and is a profound tragedy in my view: for the analysand, but also for psychoanalysis.

For me, it is not a question of whether one is pluralist or not. The question is whether one is a pluralist or totalitarian. I opt for the former, and I think so too do most psychoanalysts. Many who would claim not to be pluralists are indeed pluralists according to this definition. André Green, for example, is a good example of an analyst who works from multiple perspectives derived from studies of Freud, Klein, Bion, Winnicott, and Lacan among others. These multiple perspectives, revealed in his writing, occur at a high level of creativity. We could go round the world and name many analysts for whom this is true.

VB: How does a pluralist approach facilitate psychic transformations in the psychoanalytical process?

CB: If one has more ways of seeing mental life and human behaviour then, in my view, it follows on logically that one is going to be more effective in working with the analysand. If your preconscious stores multiple models of the mind and behaviour, to be activated by work with a particular patient in a particular moment, then you will find that you are either consciously or unconsciously envisioning the patient through one or other of these lenses. In his essay "The unconscious", Freud wrote ". . . the *Ucs.* is alive and capable of development and maintains a number of other relations with the *Pcs.*, amongst them that of co-operation" (1915e, p. 190). Analysts are facilitating the growth of the unconscious mind, and, by developing theories of the mind, establish perceptive realms in the preconscious that cooperate with the unconscious.

The analysand unconsciously knows of this co-operation between our theories and our unconscious life and *senses* this inner freedom in the psychoanalyst and as a result is more communicative. In turn, when they receive interpretations from differing views they will then internalise these perspectives and after leaving analysis they will have not only more insight into the self but *more ways of seeing* into the self and into others.

VB: Throughout your writings you return again and again to Freud's theory of free association. Indeed, in your book *Free Association* you claim that free association *grows* the unconscious: that it is mind expanding. I am sure that you are aware that many psychoanalysts regard free association as an ideal imposed by Freud that has little reality in the clinical hour. For example, it is often said that free association might be the goal of an analysis. Some would claim that many patients, borderlines for example, cannot free associate. We have to keep an eye on the theme of our conference so I also add one last comment. How is free association psychically transformative?

CB: As a preface to my comment I think it is interesting to point to one of the first references to "classical analysis". I had often wondered who it was who identified, much less promoted, classical analysis. Well, not surprisingly, it was Freud. In *The New Introductory Lectures* (1933a, p. 11) he defined the "classical method" as one in which the analyst listens to the logic of sequence presented by the analysand's narrative: "We can simply follow the chronological order in which they [the patient's utterances] appeared in the account of the dream. That is what may be called the strictest, classical method" (*ibid.*).

Perhaps we will have time to speculate on why interest in free association has diminished historically in psychoanalysis, but let me begin by saying that any patient who talks to his analyst is usually free associating. In my writings I call it "free talking" (Bollas, 2002). That simply means that the analysand talks about one thing, then another, then another, pauses now and then, and moves from one thing to another in the course of the hour. Freud regarded this movement of seemingly disparate topics as a "chain of ideas" that ultimately would reveal (in retrospect) a logic of sequence. The connecting tissues of the free associations were resident in the unconscious links between seemingly disconnected manifest contents. To get to this, the analyst must listen with an open mind. If the analyst has a selective fact blocking his listening, if he is on the edge of his seat just waiting to make a here-and-now transference interpretation, for example, he will not only never hear the free associations, he will destroy them. By interfering with his listening he will break the chain of associations and prevent the analysand from free thinking.

In *The Mystery of Things* I wrote about the psychic change wrought by the Freudian Pair and I think it is worthwhile discussing this as it bears on the theme of the conference. In brief, the dreamer returns to a foetal position, to an early form of thought, and to an early object relation, such that the dream is the mother. (Pontalis: "My hypothesis is that every dream, as an object in the analysis, refers to the maternal body", 1981, p. 29.) Every night we return to the body of our mother and we hear her oracle, which comes *as* the dream.

Freud's positioning of the patient—lying on the couch—was an uncanny intermediate stage between the sleeping thinker and the awake thinker. It is a stage between life in the world of the mother (or what I have termed the maternal order) and life in the world of the father (or what I have termed the paternal order) (Bollas, 1999, pp. 37–39).

No dreamer wants to associate to the dream. They are happy to hear the analyst's story about their dream. That does not trouble the patient's relation to his or her own dream as an object. But when the Freudian seeks to break down the whole dream by examining it in parts there is an objection. "Leave me and mama alone!"

The analyst does not, however, interrogate the patient, which would be too intrusive a violation by the paternal order.

Ingeniously, Freud asks for associations, which are somewhere between maternal and paternal orders of thought, between the dreamy world of life within the maternal ambience and the lucid world of the paternal laws and socialization.

Gradually, as the patient associates to the dream, he or she leaves the body of the mother. This is an act of separation and individuation particular to psychoanalysis. It is *based on the acquisition of knowledge*, not on some notion of the merits of socialization and maturity. When the analyst makes an interpretation, inevitably in the name of the father, this will be done only after a long period of individual development by the patient through the production of associations.

Which brings me to the second feature of psychic change. The way the Freudian analyst works with the dream is a daily act of working within the maternal and paternal orders. Over time, it accomplishes a mature pairing of the internal mother and father, and leads to *an unconscious integration of the maternal and paternal orders in the analysand*.

So, at the very heart of the analytical technique surrounding the dream we can see how dream reporting, the associations to the dream, and the interpretations of the dream are psychic transformations accomplished by the process itself.

VB: In both *The Mystery of Things* and your book *Free Association*, you pay special attention to two paragraphs from Freud's "Two encyclopaedia articles". I know you have many thoughts about these passages and I wonder, as they are brief, if you would read them and then comment on them.

CB: Sure.

First, free association: Freud writes:

> The treatment is begun by the patient being required
> to put himself in the position of an attentive and
> dispassionate self-observer, merely to read off all the
> time the surface of his consciousness, and on the one
> hand to make a duty of the most complete honesty
> while on the other not to hold back any idea from
> communication, even if (1) he feels that it is too
> disagreeable or (2) he judges that it is nonsensical or
> (3) too unimportant or (4) irrelevant to what is being
> looked for. It is uniformly found that precisely those

ideas which provoke these last-mentioned reactions
are of particular value in discovering the forgotten
material. [Freud, 1923a, p. 238]

We could spend hours discussing this. Most of us would
agree that Freud's demand for complete honesty is not possible, and this is where many analysts jump ship on the grounds
that Freud asks too much. I think the clue occurs in the last
passage, especially when he indicates that he is interested in
hearing the least relevant material.

Let's begin by determining what Freud *is not* asking for. He
is not seeking deep dark secrets. The *opposite* is true. He asks
for a narrative from the ordinary. In other words, Freud asks
to hear from the *everyday*. Out of the report of the everyday the
analysand speaks freely because there is nothing of any appar-
ent significance taking place. While analysands will hesitate to
talk about uncomfortable topics and defend against distress-
ing mental contents, the irony is that if they were to defend
against reporting the uncomfortable by supposedly talking
about something else, indeed something seemingly irrelevant,
then *over time* this talking reveals *unconscious ideas*.

VB: To interrupt you if I may, many analysts would argue that if
      the patient were consciously avoiding disclosure of something
      on the mind, then anything else they might talk about would
      be empty of significance. It would be a splitting off.

CB: Well *it could* be an empty avoidance. I do not want to categor-
      ically state that anything spoken about in order to avoid
      discussing an uncomfortable idea, experience, emotion,
      dream, or memory is inevitably freely associative. My point is
      that *if* the analysand, in an effort to escape such reporting,
      talked about what took place the previous day, paused, then
      talked about something else, then paused, then went on to talk
      about something else, that *in psychoanalytical time* he would be
      thinking unconsciously, a chain of ideas would be manifest,
      and the logic of sequence would be discoverable.

To return to the "Two encyclopaedia articles" for a moment,
it is interesting to see that Freud's identification of the
patient's task is a quintessentially modernist position and that
in this respect Freud is the psychologist of modernism. He

reflects that shift within Western culture away from vertically arranged truths—the realms of high ideas whether theological, philosophical, or high politics—to those truths found in the ordinary. It is impossible, of course, to identify a specific period of time when western culture shifted in this direction, but certainly Boswell's life of Johnson, published in 1791, is an important marking point in the humanist tradition when significance was found in the ordinary details of a life. Dickens' fiction marks a moment in the history of the English novel when the precise details of an ordinary person's life and his or her immediate surroundings found human truth. Even in the romantic poetry of Wordsworth—not far from German idealism—we see in a poem like "The Old Cumberland Beggar" exultation of the life of ordinary man.

The significant was then to be found in the realm of commonplace human life. Some would argue that the modernist tradition disappeared in the twentieth century, buried by the Holocaust. But when French historians of the 1950s, "Les annanalists", revolutionized historiography by insisting that we study the way people lived in their villages, how they married or arranged relations, traded in goods, conducted the affairs of daily life, they made the same emphasis that Freud made nearly 100 years before. Look not for what you think is the most exalted, but examine the apparently trivial or the irrelevant. The humanist and the modernist tradition survived.

I am not at all sure, however, that psychoanalysts have quite appreciated Freud's genius in this respect. For example, it is sadly not atypical of analysts, especially within the tradition of object relations to complain that if a patient is talking about matters in everyday life he or she is splitting off more hefty issues, or avoiding the transference, or something of that kind. I can discuss this in detail if we turn to the next passage, which perhaps you would kindly read.

VB: OK, this is the passage where Freud describes the analyst's task when listening to the analysand's free associations.

> Experience soon showed that the attitude which the
> analytic physician could most advantageously adopt

was to surrender himself to his own unconscious
mental activity, in a state of evenly suspended attention, to avoid so far as possible reflection and the
construction of conscious expectations, not to try to
fix anything he heard particularly in his memory, and
by these means to catch the drift of the patient's
unconscious with his own unconscious. [*ibid.*, p. 239]

CB: Let me repeat the last phrase because I think every psychoanalyst should put this on the wall and read it every day. ". . .
and by these means to catch the drift of the patient's unconscious with his own unconscious". The primary agency of the
work of psychoanalysis is *unconscious*! Indeed, it is unconscious to unconscious. This is not the only time Freud makes
this kind of statement, as we know. Indeed, in his *crucial* essay
"On beginning the treatment" in 1913, he has already written
"while I am listening to the patient, I, too, give myself over to
the current of my unconscious thoughts" (Freud, 1913, p. 134).
     Let us take notice of his definition of the analyst's frame of
mind. The psychoanalyst should "surrender himself to his
own unconscious mental activity". Well, those of you who are
into Zen may take note that these are not the words of a Zen
master, but of Freud, who makes it very clear here that, so far
as the observing ego is concerned, one must abandon it in
order to surrender to one's own unconscious. Unlike Zen,
Freud does not privilege this moment because it empties the
mind. He is aware that this action allows for unconscious
reception on his part and he will learn something, but it will
be learned through unconscious processes of thought. Let us
note further what he says. The analyst is "to avoid reflection".
He is to avoid, so far as possible, "the construction of conscious expectations" and, finally, he is to "try not to fix anything he heard particularly in his memory". So, he is to avoid
reflection, expectation, and memory.
     We have Bion before Bion.
     I term Freud's definition of the free associating analysand
and the evenly suspended analyst "the Freudian Pair" in
recognition of the revolutionary discovery of a new object
relation. Looked at in terms of the phylogenetic needs of the

human being, the Freudian Pair is a huge step forward in our object relations and in the creative use of unconscious processes of thought.

Although, fortunately, for many psychoanalysts the Freudian Pair is the centrepiece of their clinical imagination and they learn from the analysand, it is also true, in my view, that too many analysts have shoved this technique aside and dismissed it.

I learned a great deal from my supervisors in ego psychology in the USA and from Kleinians and object relational theorists in England. These groups do not work with this model. Typically, in supervision with an ego psychologist, I would be asked as I reported the session to describe the ego's position. If I made a comment, I would be asked to what part of the ego the comment had been addressed and how and in what ways the ego was mediating id derivatives and superego psychic actions. Where were the compromise formations? In England, later, I would be asked *always* about the transference. How and in what ways was the patient referring to myself?

The point of this observation is that at least as they teach—and teaching or supervising is a hazardous activity in psychoanalysis—these analysts had an agenda. I was meant to be very alert and highly determined to find what they reckoned I should find. The idea that I was to listen without reflection, anticipation, or memory was off the map.

VB: In fact, if I understand from what you have said earlier, you think that some analytical techniques actually prevent unconscious communication from taking place.

CB: Sadly this is true. If the analyst has it in mind that he or she is going to interpret the transference in the here and now, then they are not practising psychoanalysis even remotely related to the Freudian proposal. So, too, for analysts who are thinking they must listen to the ego's positionings, or the work of the castration complex, or whatnot. The bizarre thing, in my view, is that analysts will say that if they cannot follow the patient's narrative then either it is an "evacuation" or "an attack on linking" or they feel "flooded" by the material. In fact, Freud's proposal is that one *should not* be following the meanings as they are uttered. Indeed, if the patient moves from one topic to another, the manifest content somewhat disconnected, then the analysand is actually engaged in unconscious thinking. Time and again analysts will report that because they cannot follow the manifest content they feel there is an attack on linking.

In fact, the patient is thinking!

The links that matter to Freud are the *unconscious links* and, if the word *unconscious* is to have any meaning, we must mean that therefore the links are not consciously understood *in situ* by the psychoanalyst. Only *later* when the logic of sequence asserts itself—and I think for Freud this is a kind of revelation in consciousness when consciousness is suddenly informed by unconscious perception—can the analyst discover the links.

VB: Is it not possible, however, that some of these selected facts that analysts have in mind while with patients, are really more like forms of transitional object? They might be thinking of looking for the transference, or observing the ego, or tracking the castration complex and drive derivatives, but might it not be the case that these mental objects are the means through which these clinicians can widen their view in the course of time?

CB: This may be so. I think if an analyst has a favoured object in mind—and you mentioned some of the possibilities—then theory functions as a fetish. It is a defence against the castration anxiety proposed by the analytical encounter. Of course, this encounter can elicit castration anxiety, especially if you aim to try to dominate the analysand through your analytical work, and if so you will of necessity need your fetish in order to engage in some form of intercourse with the analysand.

VB: So are you arguing that many psychoanalysts are no longer working within the unconscious?

CB: What has happened, over time, is that analysts have moved the goal posts and are now working with models that assume the analyst's consciousness can observe, grasp, or interpret the analysand's unconscious *in situ*. I submit this is psychologically possible only if one removes the theory of the unconscious from our minds. Unfortunately, the *tacit assumptions* of many psychoanalysts reveal an abandonment of belief in unconscious processes.

I think we are living now within the Theocracy of Consciousness. We find in this new state a form of hypertrophied consciousness with the analyst functioning as a kind of God. He or she is at best an observing God—aware of all that is taking place—or an interpreting God, but none the less a God who has fetishistic objects to accompany the act of domination of the analysand. I am afraid the transference has gone to our heads in more ways than one.

VB: From a clinical point of view how can one make use of Freud's statement? I am quite sure that some colleagues present would feel that you were calling for a kind of detachment, or believing in perhaps some kind of mystical connection to the patient. I would have thought, also, that some colleagues would state that Freud's position in 1923 is certainly contradicted by other writings of his and that as we have learned more about the transference and more about character disorders, the borderline for example, that Freud's evenly suspended model is a nice idea, but an ideal at best and perhaps its own delusion. So, I am sorry to focus on the issue of "clinical evidence", but actually what evidence do you have that the Freudian Pair generates the chains of ideas that Freud proposes?

CB: Well, in the first place, this is the way I have always worked. Regardless of the analysand—and it does not matter whether the person is neurotic, borderline, or schizophrenic—all people free associate. You see, Freud's theory of free association is actually—if we think about it—a theory of mental life. When we think about things to ourselves we move from one thing to another to another in an endless sequelae of thoughts. So we think associatively.

In *Studies On Hysteria*, when Freud follows a particular line of thought, he alludes to its remarkable density and complexity. He writes, "The logical chain corresponds not only to a zig-zag, twisted line, but rather to a ramifying system of lines and more particularly to a converging one. It contains nodal points at which two or more threads meet and thereafter proceed as one" (1895d, p. 290). In the Dream Book, when looking at one simple short dream—the dream of the botanical monograph—he is clearly taken by how the image of the botanical monograph "was linked with the psychically significant event by copious associative connections". He reveals his astonishment. "Not only the compound idea, 'botanical monograph', however, but each of its components, 'botanical' and 'monograph' separately, led by numerous connecting paths deeper and deeper into the tangle of dream-thoughts" (*ibid.*, p. 282). In the same paragraph he concludes, "Thus 'botanical' was a regular nodal point in the dream. Numerous trains of thought converged upon it . . . [and I jump ahead to the conclusion] . . . we find ourselves in a factory of thought where, as in the 'weaver's masterpiece' [and now he quotes a stanza from Goethe, the last two lines of which I quote] 'Unseen the threads are knit together / And an infinite combination grows'" (*ibid.*).

So. Our unconscious is a dynamic factory of thought that knits together "infinite" lines of thought that combine and grow. Some of the lines come together for a while and create nodal points, and because of their increased psychic weight may come into consciousness, but all along, of course, there are thousands and thousands of other lines of thought in this ramifying factory that continue separately.

This infinite combination of growing thought is, in my view, Freud's core theory of the unconscious and clearly a model of mental development.

So, to go back to your question, from a theoretical point of view it is simply not possible that people cannot free associate because that is akin to saying they have no unconscious life, and unless they are brain dead they have one.

The issue, however, as I think you pose, is how can the psychoanalyst have access to these lines of thought? I think this is something that, within limits, we can study, and we can improve our unconscious capabilities as analysts if we understand that many of us have been in resistance to the Freudian Pair. If we reopen our minds to Freud's proposal we can meet, discuss sessions, and see *afterwards* how sessions indicate lines of thought. We may see how the mind thinks in a sequential logic—albeit many ideas simultaneously, but some more weighty than others.

I have met with groups of about twenty-five analysts for some ten years. One group in Stockholm and the other in either Zurich or Tübingen. [These groups have now joined to form ESGUT, the European Study Group of Unconscious Thought. VB]. We study processed sessions in detail and examine how the analysand's narrative order follows a chain of ideas that, on reflection, reveals the logic of latent mental contents. Of course, this is cheating in a way, because we go over the sessions again and again, freezing unconscious articulation in a limited time-frame, but by this means it is possible to discover differing lines of thought. It allows us to see how a patient is at work all by himself or herself.

One of the most intriguing aspects of our work is the discovery that most analysands ask either explicit or implicit questions in sessions. It is as if there is an epistemophilic drive that poses unconscious questions and works out unconscious answers. Indeed, almost invariably when a patient asks an explicit question the very next topic answers the question. One can point this out to the analysand and in this way rather introduce them to *their* own unconscious.

Work at this level is quite ordinary. One simply applies Freud's theory of "ab". He writes

> In a psychoanalysis one learns to interpret propinquity in time as representing connection in subject-matter. Two thoughts that occur in immediate sequence without any apparent connection are in fact part of a single unity which has to be discovered; in just the same way, if I write an "*a*" and a "*b*" in succession, they have to be pronounced as a single syllable "*ab*". [1900a, p. 247]

So, if a patient begins a session and says that last night her daughter did not return home on time and goes into some detail and is then quiet and says that she does not know why she is so anxious today, it is possible to see that by "ab" (Freud's theory of sequential contiguity) she is linking the daughter's not being at home on time and her anxiety the next day. One need only follow such lines of thought in sessions— of course they are inevitably much more complex than this and unconsciously grasped by the analyst—to make a comment on what seems to be most significant.

VB: So the groups of analysts with whom you have been working have discovered that in every case, of every session, that the analysand freely associates?

CB: No. The most frequent problem, certainly in the beginning of our work, was that an overly active psychoanalyst—especially one making interpretations in the beginning of the hour—destroyed the prospect of free association.

VB: So you are saying that it is the analyst who prevents free association from emerging?

CB: That is the most common reason. The analyst *intervenes* and incarcerates the analysand's unconscious thinking long enough to throw things off. Then both patient and analyst are in a state of resistance to unconscious communication.

VB: Surely you cannot be arguing, however, that there are no cases in which the patient is resistant to free association, such that in effect it is not taking place?

CB: No, of course not. Freud was clear that if a patient's free associations were too copious and the analyst felt that he was being lead on some kind of lost expedition that this would be evidence of a resistance to free association. The silent patient who refuses to speak clearly resists the reporting of free associations although they will be occurring internally. Perhaps the most common resistance, however, is vague articulation: the patient who speaks in abstract language devoid of detail. But here, too, one often finds that the analyst is also interested in highly abstract reporting and not interested in the psychic value of reported everydayness.

VB: Have you ever met a patient who, however much they tried, could not free associate?

CB: I certainly have met analysands who initially could not free associate. For a while I did not know what to do. But one patient—a psychoanalyst who felt ashamed and illegitimate that she practised analysis but had never associated in her analysis—was indeed seized up and this was a problem. At best she would talk about one or another colleagues, or some work she was doing, but then she would stop and panic. Although we analysed the sources of her panic, which I cannot go into here, one day I realized that you cannot associate to a dream if you do not have a dream and then my next thought was that you cannot have a dream if you have not had lived experience in the day (equivalent to saying you cannot dream if you have not been alive). So, at the beginning of a session when she seized up, I said please tell me what happened yesterday, begin with the beginning and go through the day. She asked "why?". I said I thought that by recollecting the day's events thoughts would follow. So she began, but not in detail. She said after the last session she had gone shopping and then she went for coffee. I interrupted her and said could she please slow down and tell me which shop she went into. She said it was a shoe store and then went on to talk about the coffee, but I stopped her again and said could she please slow down and tell me the name of the store, the names of the shoes, and so forth. Now, she is an intelligent person and so she got the gist of this, and for the next fifteen minutes or so she described exactly what she had done, what she had seen, and then, as she began talking about a moment when she had to take her car for repair (yes, an interesting moment in the story), she drifted off and talked about events from the previous week, then other events in her life. In other words, she began free associating. From that moment she was able to do it and of course we discussed this, and I put to her what I have said here: that it was too much to expect her to free associate without speaking from within her lived experience.

VB: Do you consider that analysis, however? Some would argue that your intervention was remedial and that you avoided those issues that operated according perhaps to −K or that you performed a kind of psychotherapy.

CB: I certainly accept that this was a form of psychotherapy and not psychoanalysis. The word psychotherapy does have a special meaning and function within the practise of psychoanalysis because I think analysts do psychotherapy now and then with their patients. It is actually meant to be rather shameful because it smacks of the effort to actually intervene and help the patient. To this I plead guilty. But if the patient's associations were operating under the auspices of −K, which, as it turned out, they were not, then I would still have listened to the associative logic according to −K.

VB: Even if you understood that what the patient was saying was devoted to the denudation of meaning? How would you work with such a function?

CB: I do not think that unconscious thinking in itself could function according to −K. That said, some part of the patient's ego has made the unconscious decision to use speech as antithought. And if the patient is reading you the telephone directory or . . .

VB: If I may . . . or if the patient is talking to you about everyday experience from −K?

CB: Yes, if the patient is talking to me from −K they would still be free associating, even if such associations were simultaneously subjected by the patient to −K. We are addressing at this conference psychic transformations, so if the analysand is thinking in −K and if the units of thought are beta, I will none the less listen for the chain of ideas—which would always be there even if of no interest to the patient—and I would always seek to bring them to his or her attention. We need not only think of the more radical examples. In contemporary culture there is contempt towards the mind and the unconscious and most people are not interested in knowing what they think unconsciously. It takes a lot of work for the psychoanalyst to introduce the patient to his own unconscious mind.

However, we are talking here only about free association. Mental life continues no matter how it is understood by the analysand. If the patient was functioning in −K I would address that function within the transference or I would make a character interpretation. In other words, simply because free association can be observed to take place does not mean that one should interpret the chain of ideas because many other things may be happening that would take clinical priority.

VB: But you are saying that no matter the diagnostic category or the destructive intentions of the analysand if he or she is talking about their life, moving from one event to another, that chains of ideas will emerge and you would or could bring them to the patient's attention?

CB: Yes.

VB: But what about the transference and the interpretation of it? Or what about the character formations and how the patient speaks through enactment? Or what about projective processes and how the patient projectively identifies something into objects? Or indeed, what about the flow of affects in the session. Do you simply ignore these dimensions? I don't think you do, but you can see that this question has to be asked?

CB: Of course I see the necessity of this question. Our discussion has narrowed to only one dimension of the analysand's communications: to the line of logic revealed through narrative. We are talking about it and I am writing about it only because appreciation of this dimension is disappearing from psychoanalysis and so I concentrate on it for those reasons only. But there are other lines of articulation: affects and object relations, for example. Each of these lines of expression can be addressed within its own category. There are different types of expression that belong either to respectively different categories, or use multiple categories for articulation. The transference is one order of thinking that I would put under the category of the relational, but it also articulates itself through the categories of affect, body gesture, and so forth.

VB: You have said earlier and just now that you believe our understanding of free association is disappearing from psychoanalysis. Why do you think this is so?

CB: We could spend hours on this, so I must be woefully brief. In the very first place, Freud did not write enough about this because he *assumed* it and assumptions are dangerous intellectual actions. Second, Freud had several different theories of how we listen to narrative content as evidence of unconscious thought. His theory of repression proposes that the narrative is a manifest text that will rupture at points where a derepressed content emerges, whether that is a parapraxis or the affective investment of a phrase that invests it with more significance.

VB: Have you always found free association of interest?

CB: Well you can't study and teach English literature unless you know how to follow the line of logic in a narrative sequence. It is impossible, for example, to examine a poem without starting at the beginning and then discovering how the poet's sequence of ideas presents a series of statements, sometimes of great complexity. I studied psychoanalytic literary criticism at the University of Buffalo and we were trained to read the logic of sequence in all narratives: plays, novels, or poems. It takes some training, but because it is the way we think anyway (that is, in a psychological sequence of associations), it is more a matter of bringing into the preconscious a model of how the unconscious works. Then it is not difficult to bring this into analytical practice.

VB: A moment ago you mentioned categories and I am not sure that everyone here will know how much emphasis you put on "category errors", which is a concept from the English philosopher Gilbert Ryle.

CB: Ryle's work is very important, in my view, because he helps us to see how we must be sure that when we discuss in our case, for example, theory, that we are not mixing categories. In his book *The Concept of Mind* (1949), Ryle gives three examples of what he terms a category error. A man is touring a university and has looked at all the buildings but asks his host, "Where is the university?" "He was mistakenly allocating the university to the same category as that to which the other institutions belong" (*ibid.*, p. 18), explains Ryle. A child watches a division of soldiers passing by—battalions, batteries, squadrons, etc.—but asks afterwards when the division was going to show up? A foreigner is watching a cricket match and the game is explained to him, but he asks, "But where is the team spirit?" Ryle explains, "He was looking for the wrong type of thing" (*ibid.*).

Later, Ryle turns to how different principles can be applied to the same observed phenomena. One could, according to Ryle, examine a literary text and note "the grammatical rules which its word-arrangements observe, the stylistic canons which its word-arrangements observe, and the logical rules which its word-arrangements observe" (*ibid.*, p. 77). Ryle claims that there is no conflict between these different "types of principles" and he adds "all alike are applied in the same material; all alike can supply licences for correct predictions; all alike may be referred to for answers to questions of the same verbal pattern" (*ibid.*).

Strictly speaking, Ryle's theory of a category error illustrates how an observer looking at things—university buildings, cricket players, a marching division—confuses the concrete objects with their mental conceptualizations. I think his theory of "types of principles", however, allows us to expand his concept of a category error. An error need not be about concrete thinking. A person can simply be looking for the wrong thing in the wrong place.

VB: Earlier you said that there were many different forms of unconscious expression, indicating that when you think of free association it operates in different categories.

CB: I think of the unconscious—that is, I imagine it—through two images. First, the image of a symphonic score.

Imagine that the temporal movement of the analysand's discourses is a horizontal axis, from left to right, from the beginning of the session to the end of the hour. Then imagine a vertical axis that consists of different categories of unconscious presentation or representation. Each of these categories has its own line of movement—its own logic if you will—and often they will converge to create nodal points, but they are not the same.

A single word—travelling in the phonemic category—may utter many things.

A patient uses the word "helicopter". Imagine this word on a line and below the line are listed the signifiers that drop out of this word, so to speak, and above the line are the cultural signifieds that emanate from the word. So, out of the word we get other words dropping down: "hell", "I", "cop", "copt", and "her". Above the line you get images of war, of a chopper, of it flying, and perhaps of television coverage, plus whatever else occurs to you. Not all words, but many, have this vertical potential, and as the analysand speaks there will be an incredible networking of differing word meanings. Lacanian analysis privileges the chain of signifiers. Object relations theory privileges the chain of images. As an aside, this word proved significant in the analysis of a man because it actually contained a meaning related to his aggressive treatment of women: "Hell I copt her".

Now let us turn to some of the other categories on the vertical axis.

Psychoanalysis is largely auditory. We listen the voice of the patient. A line of thought is articulated through the sound of the speaker's voice. On the vertical axis we could have a category, the sonic. That category would allow us to designate qualities such as "i" for irony, "s" for sarcasm, "r" for resignation and so on and so on.

Another category is the analysand's use of the analytic object. This is the movement of the analysand's idiom—or aesthetic of being—that uses the many instruments in analysis, such that he or she leaves a trace of their being. It is like the signature of Mozart or Bruckner, the idiom or form of his or her own styles of musical thinking.

Transference as a category is obvious, isn't it? This would indicate the category of transference and the line of transference *thinking*. I emphasize transference as a form of thinking because enactment is a form of thought and so transference is the use of the analytical object.

There would be a category of projective identification. Here one identifies the line of projective thinking, the realm of object relations. It is certainly possible to see the analysand's material in these terms.

Use of the object, transference, projective identification, though distinct, are part of the larger category, the relational. So, let's term the larger class a category and those forms of expression that are part of the larger class an order. We have the categories language, sonic, body, and the relational that have separate orders that may follow their own particular lines of thought (i.e., transference) or may join other categories, as when a person expresses an idea sonically, gesturally, and transferentially. The expression "get out of here!" would do just that.

One could use Bion's L, H, and K as notations that would signify mental qualities moving within the material of mental life.

If we imagine each category as a symbolic musical instrument—one the violin, the other the flute—then the symphonic metaphor becomes richer because you can see something of how the instruments play at different times, sometimes joining others, sometimes alone, sometimes all of a piece—but separately—and, although I do not want to stretch the metaphor beyond credibility (and perhaps I am doing so), I none the less think it helps us to see that there is some form of *orchestration* to unconscious thinking.

It is very important to bear in mind that simply because one of these categories is momentarily silent this does not mean that it ceases to exist. Freud wrote of the "unobjectionable" transference. This simply means that at any moment in time there is relatively little conflict in the transference, so it is silent. Of course, transference issues will always be there as memories, just as with a symphonic work one can recall the sound of the flutes in a previous passage even if now they are silent.

Well, I can't go any further with this now as I only want to indicate *some*, by no means all, categories that constitute the movement of unconscious thinking and unconscious creativity.

VB: You said that you had another metaphor—other than the symphonic one—that you use.

CB: Yes, it is the image of a map. I use this for teaching purposes as it helps newcomers to appreciate the density of the unconscious. So, imagine a map of the United States (and of course you could pick any country or even the world, but I shall try to keep this simple). As you hear a word, see which localities pop into mind.

I mention the word "jazz" and right away you will find a kind of connecting line, certainly with New Orleans perhaps in the middle, but in my mind, if moving horizontally from west to east, it would start in San Francisco, move to Austin, Texas, up to Chicago, down to New Orleans, and then north to New York City, and finally Boston. These are the great jazz epicentres in the US.

Imagine now that I mention the phrase "mountain retreat". Again moving from west to east, one might start with Mount Lassen in northern California, move south to Tahoe, east to the Rockies, then to small villages in the Appalachians: south and north.

Imagine that I mention the word "festival". Again we could cross the USA from west to east, and I won't detail this, as I am sure you begin to get the picture.

So, now imagine that the analysand says the following: "I would like to go to a jazz festival in some mountain retreat".

My view is that with each word there is an immediate map in the analysand's and the analyst's mind. The sentence creates overlapping maps—like Freud's imagined zig-zagging, criss-crossing lines of thought—and then, at least for the patient, there might be a nodal point, such as Aspen, Colorado, where there is a festival that includes well-known jazz groups, and is a mountain retreat.

The point is that as the analysand speaks on and on in the hour, hundreds of such maps are evoked and are latently active. They constitute a matrix for that analysand in his analysis.

Of course, the map I have drawn is only a didactic tool, because any psychic map would be *very* different. Imagine a patient for whom the word "jazz" linked to agitated oral sexual life, that "festival" evoked the image of a huge feast, that "resort" evoked the sorting centre of a post office, so the point of convergence would be a different map. It might condense into an image of a post office in Rio. That could be a dream image for the night. Or it could be a free association in the session. Or if he were a novelist it could be the first lines of a novel.

The map is an example of thinking within the category of the imaginary. [See Chapter Two. CB.]

VB: This borders on your theory of unconscious creativity.

CB: Yes, because although the repressed unconscious is one important theory of unconscious thinking it is far too narrow a perspective and does not accord with Freud's theory of dreamwork, which is a theory of unconscious creativity. Our minds are far too complex to be about any one thing, be it a repressed idea, an id derivative, the transference, or anything. Indeed, at any moment in psychic time, if we could have a look at the unconscious symphony it would be a vast network of creative combinations.

I have proposed that along with the concept of the repressed unconscious we consider the *received unconscious* (see Bollas, 1987, pp. 239–240, 1989, p. 202, 1992, pp. 66–100, 1995, p. 31). The received would initially be constituted out of thing impressions that congregate in the unconscious and draw to them further thing presentations that form nuclei in the unconscious. They become condensations of thousands of experiences and as we live and think, in time, our mind grows. The receptive unconscious stores unconscious perceptions, it organizes them, and it is the matrix of creativity. It also includes the repressed unconscious, which operates according to its own laws. This is a theory of unconscious perception based upon what interests us. In the Dream Book, when discussing the impressions of the day (where he examines the dream of the botanical monograph) Freud discusses a very "*important* impression" that was of "a high degree of psychical importance", which he then says, "had justifiably stirred my feelings" (Freud, 1900a, p. 174). Elsewhere Freud does link this to a theory of affective perception of reality, but although, to my knowledge, Freud never discusses a theory of unconscious perception, he does use one, and indeed it is vital to the concept of the receptive unconscious.

I think his telephone metaphor *is* a theory of the receptive unconscious. As you know, in his "Recommendations to physicians practising psycho-analysis" (1912e), he identified the type of unconscious thought needed to listen to the patient in the state of evenly suspended attentiveness. He wrote: "To put it in a formula: he must turn his own unconscious like a receptive organ towards the transmitting unconscious of the patient. He must adjust himself to the patient as a telephone receiver is adjusted to the transmitting microphone" (pp. 115–116). And he proceeds to discuss how "the receiver" works. Now, this is *not* the unconscious of the repressed unconscious. It is a different theory of the unconscious, a theory of unconscious perception.

Those of you who are interested in Freud's theory of the dream and who are interested in his *other* theory of the unconscious—his theory of reception—will appreciate that he never put this theory in one place: it is strung out in his writings, appearing here and there, rather like the return of the repressed unconscious! In *Being a Character* I wrote about internal organizations in the unconscious that I termed "psychic genera", and this was very much based on Freud's idea of thing presentations. If you have a look at the Dream Book, part one, page 175, you will find Freud providing a perfect example of what I term the evocative object that calls up an unconscious matrix.

He is discussing associations of a dreamer to a friend's "smoked salmon". It was the friend's "favourite dish" and Freud then concludes that "the friend's favourite dish . . . was an immediate constituent of the group of ideas which were likely to be aroused in the dreamer's mind by the personality of her friend" (Freud, 1900a, p. 175). In this single half sentence Freud proposes a *profound* concept of how we think: that as we think of people or places or events they are always linked to a group of ideas (whether we recall them or not) and it is this movement of the groups of ideas, or matrices of thought, that I believe best characterizes how we think.

Of course, this network is operated by the ego. It is the ego that dreams the dream, that thinks the free associations, that also writes the novels, creates symphonies, and so forth.

VB: Is this the ego of ego psychology?

CB: It is the ego as Freud identified it in his theory of the primary repressed unconscious and the work of the ego as the *other* unconscious, when he bumped up against his own category error in *The Ego and the Id*, but fortunately enough he knew it and recognized it. One theory, of course, was that of the repressed mental contents, but then he noted that the agency that did the repressing was also unconscious, so which one was the real unconscious? It was only a category error, but one that has had a rather long effect on psychoanalysis.

You will recall at the end of Chapter One of *The Ego and the Id* that Freud is somewhat despondent about having found this supposedly new unconscious. "When we find ourselves thus confronted by the necessity of postulating a third *Ucs.*, which is not repressed," he writes, "we must admit that the characteristic of being unconscious begins to lose significance for us." He then writes of how the unconscious would appear to have too many qualities, but in the very last sentence he pulls back from his despair to firmly announce "Nevertheless we must beware of ignoring this characteristic, for the property of being conscious or not is in the last resort our one beacon-light in the darkness of depth-psychology" (Freud, 1923b, p. 18). If *only* he had realized that he had confused content with process. There were and are, of course, repressed mental contents. There are many differing kinds of dynamic unconscious processes—just think of the difference between writing a musical work and writing a novel for example—and Freud's remarkable theory of how a dream is formed through the day into the night is in itself one such remarkable unconscious process.

Ego psychology, *per se*, became a movement with a particular and, in my view, a valued perspective on Freud, but one that was of necessity limited. I actually think Hartmann's works are profound as well as the work of David Rapaport and George Klein. I think the theories of neutralization, of the conflict-free area, and of sublimation are valid *within limits*. One needs to know actually what part of the pie they are addressing.

They were obviously not interested in free association and I can find no references in their work to anything like the theory of unconscious communication. Read Greenson and those who follow and you will not find the Freud, who argues that the analyst listens to the patient's unconscious with his own unconscious.

To be fair, they were working in different categories. In *The Mind in Conflict* (1982), Charles Brenner never mentions free association, but I would be committing a category error if I were to lament its absence, as I think Brenner was working in a *different and important* area of theory, one that really pivots around the structural model.

Freud's theory of the unconscious that I prefer was obviously not to their taste. And, as Freud was in perpetual conflict and in contradiction with himself, anyone—including, of course, myself—can find his or her favourite Freud to quote.

VB: I would like to clarify something you have said about the logic of sequence. In a single session, presumably one or maybe two lines of thought emerge through the chain of ideas. As you are arguing that the unconscious itself is a vast network of differing orders of thinking, how do you explain what really amounts to a reduction of its complexity within the hour?

CB: First, remember that there are differing categories of unconscious expression, so they are functioning in different ways than simply in narrative sequence. In *Free Association* I also write about different narrative "wavelengths", because some chains of ideas occur over weeks, months, or more. But to come to the heart of your point, how is it possible to discover such a chain within an hour? I think that the unconscious knows where it is. I think it knows the difference between the psychoanalyst and a taxi driver, symphony conductor, or plumber. As such, analysands unconsciously present and represent those symptoms, conflicts, character dilemmas that have troubled them, so they set about working with us. I think it is also interesting to notice that there is a certain kind of psychic pace to each analysand, a way that they take time working on several issues. Clearly those lines of thought that are ready to come into consciousness *after* a period of unconscious work between analysand and analyst are those that come closer to the surface and are more easily perceived by the psychoanalyst.

In my book on free association, however, I point out that I think Freud's theory of interpretation derives from a sense of surprise. He suddenly sees a logic of sequence. Something strikes him. In Dora, he discusses this in a footnote. He asks Dora to pay close attention to "the exact words" that she used, but in the footnote he tells us why. "I laid stress on these words," he writes, "because they took me aback" (Freud, 1905e, p. 65). All analysts will recognize these moments. After a long period of unconscious reception of the analysand's material we are surprised by something in particular, and usually that announces unconscious comprehension now coming into consciousness. We *then* concentrate on something particular.

VB: To return to the theme of the conference, how does the symphonic metaphor or the map metaphor help us understand psychic transformations within the process?

CB: I think each generation of analysts must refresh the models of the unconscious so that we are forced to think it for ourselves. If we simply rest on past conceptualizations they then become *assumptions*, and the problem with assumptions is that one no longer thinks about the assumed or the received truth.

Further, I think it allows us to reinvent the Freudian ego, to return to Freud's dream theory as the example of ego work, and to see how the symphony of the unconscious—coordinated by this ego—stages an extraordinary range of interests and conflicts. We are less likely, it seems to me, to be limited to identifying the one theme of an hour or a week, whether it be the unconscious phantasy of the hour, or the ego issue of the hour, or the transference theme. Even if each of these concentrations is valid, this can only be up to a point, as there are far more conflicts—or convergences of the conflicted— than we can see at any moment in time.

Remembering Freud's remarkable statement—the "analyst catches the patient's unconscious with his own unconscious"—stresses the work of unconscious thinking. What comes into consciousness will, of course, be highly relevant to the work of psychoanlysis, but we should not be so enamoured with how much we consciously comprehend of our patients.

VB: I want to thank you for your participation in this interview, which has indeed been wide ranging. I think it has dealt, in many respects, with the theme of this conference.

CB: It has been a pleasure.

CHAPTER TWO

Articulations of the unconscious

VB: You return to Freud's theory of the logic of narrative sequence because he believed this is one way that unconscious thinking is revealed. *Why* do you stress this particular point in his theory?

CB: Although Freud never proposed a theory of unconscious perception, his concept of the formation of a dream is impossible without it. I refer to the unconscious that registers "psychically valuable" experiences during the day, collects them into "complexes", condenses them into the dream, and then remembers them the following day. Ironically enough, his theory of unconscious perception would seem to be unconscious! This theory of the unconscious never entered his metapsychology. Yet, the startling one-liner in his essay "The unconscious" (1915e) —"It is a very remarkable thing that the Ucs. of one human being can react upon that of another, without passing through the Cs" (p. 194)—can only be a return of the repressed.

VB: What has been repressed?

CB: Freud repressed *knowledge* of his mother, and with this repressed *form* of love he was now unconscious of the mother's contribution to the self's psychic structure. The repressed returns almost as a parapraxal slip in his main essay on the unconscious, where he devotes himself to an altogether paternalistic theory of the unconscious as the forbidden thought.

The forbidden statement ("a remarkable thing . . .") directs attention to a relationship where one human being "react[s] upon that of another" without knowledge of this contact passing through consciousness. We know *this* relation to be the one between mother and infant. Freud's statement, therefore, constitutes a return of the repressed, within the *act* of writing.

The unconscious formed between infant and mother and later toddler and mother, occurs, in Freudian theory, *before* the repressed unconscious. It is the era of the construction of the self's psychic architecture. Maternal communication—a processional logic—informs the infant's world view. What is known cannot be thought, yet constitutes the foundational knowledge of one's self: the "unthought known". Freud knew this because his theory of the thing-presentation conceptualizes the preverbal world's effect upon the self. These effects become psychic areas; memories of being and relating now become assumptions about living. These areas associate to one another and develop the matrix of the unconscious. This matrix constitutes the primary repressed unconscious or the self's ego. As always we must bear in mind that the primary thing-presenter is the maternal unconscious that communicates itself in innumerable ways, notably through its processional logic: that is, as a transformational object.

The "ego" names a process—unconscious organization—that develops its history from that logic. By the time the child is capable of repression he has already formed unconscious means of organizing and communicating his experiences of life. More can be said about this, but Freud's entire theory of primary repression discusses this unconscious even though it is not included in his metapsychology.

Freud's Dream Book, testimony to him of his life's work, however, may be an offering to the mother's informative knowledge. It is adequately disguised (he does not dare conceptualize a theory of unconscious perception as this would deny the paternal law to the censor) and thereby escapes paternal attention. This most revolutionary book, written after the death of his father, does not, therefore, triumph over the paternal order because relation to the maternal order (i.e., "intercourse with the mother") is repressed. Freud is free to celebrate the father and the function of censorship. An identification has supplemented the act of repression.

VB: So Freud's theory of repression, ironically enough, represses his other theory of the unconscious.

CB: Exactly. Repression, an important part of the unconscious, is by no means the most substantial part. Freud fails to conceptualize his realization. He begins the essay on "The Unconscious" with the following observation: "Everything that is repressed must remain unconscious; but let us state at the very outset that the repressed does not cover everything that is unconscious (166)." As if this observation needs further emphasis he immediately adds "The unconscious has a wider compass: the repressed is a part of the unconscious (167)." He does not, however, address this wider unconscious. How is it formed? What is its status within the system unconscious? Freud has shackled himself to a theory of the repressed unconscious that he knows is not inclusive of all that constitutes the dynamic unconscious. The topographic model is constructed around this internal father—as censor—so that only the theory of the repressed unconscious is articulated. One of the casualties of his limited view is the pleasure of unconscious perception. During an ordinary day we please ourselves all the time as we construct matrices from lived experience, memories, and sexual and aggressive drives.

VB: In our earlier discussion you used Freud's theory of the preconscious to discuss where we store models of the mind. I had wanted to ask you about this, especially as, in your concept of the received unconscious, you seem to have found a different term to describe what you mean.

CB: Just as Freud referred to the unconscious in its descriptive as well as its dynamic sense, so, too, does his theory of the preconscious have a descriptive as well as a dynamic meaning. I believe the dynamic preconscious relates only to the censorship of unacceptable ideas. It is an important point of view and crucial to conceiving the fate of repressed ideas. At the same time, however, there is a non-dynamic preconscious that refers simply to all those previously conscious ideas that are not presently conscious. In our Athens discussion I did indeed refer to the analyst's internalization of ideas as occupying the analyst's preconscious, as I did not want to complicate matters further, then, by referring to my own theory of the receptive unconscious.

VB: How does the receptive unconscious differ from the preconscious?

CB: If we move beyond the descriptive to the dynamic, then the preconscious would refer to that part of the unconscious that processes the return of unwanted ideas. There is a particular psychic work involved in passing unwanted thoughts back into consciousness in derivative form, and Freud's theory of the preconscious addresses this unconscious task. But his theory of the dream work implicitly recognizes a dynamic unconscious that operates through categories of reception and representation that are not determined by censorship. Indeed, although I think the topographic model should be retained, I believe the theory of the preconscious is faulty. We do not need a second form of the unconscious to account for the work accomplished by the preconscious. In any event, one can see Freud fudging the precise status of the preconscious. Ultimately, if we regard this as simply a name for a type of action undertaken by the unconscious, then I believe we avoid the pitfalls Freud created for himself by trying to come up with a second type of unconscious.

VB: The receptive unconscious seems to recognize a different type of unconscious process.

CB: Exactly. But to follow on from what we have just discussed, it is not a separate unconscious from the unconscious that represses unwanted ideas. Unconscious organization is capable of both receiving or repressing ideas. I pay special attention, however, to its receptive function, because this has not been adequately conceptualized. What I term the receptive unconscious must be the unconscious to which Freud refers in the 1923 essay describing evenly suspended attentiveness

(1923a), when the analyst catches the drift of his patient's unconscious with his own unconscious. He is surely not here talking about the unconscious of the topographic model. For were this to be so, it would mean that in listening the analyst would subject the material to his or her own unconscious distortion. In "Recommendations to physicians practising psycho-analysis" (1912e), he has already made it clear that the analyst's unconscious is indeed receptive. He actually uses this word. "To put it in a formula he must turn his own unconscious like a *receptive* organ towards the transmitting unconscious of the patient: (*ibid.*, p. 115 [my italics]). He continues that "the doctor's unconscious is able, from the derivatives of the unconscious which are communicated to him, to reconstruct that unconscious, which has determined the patient's free associations" (*ibid.*, p. 116). Once again, *this* unconscious is unconscious perception. It is a highly organized means of receiving a transmitted message. Neither the process nor the contents are congruent here with his theory of repression or the repressed unconscious. Of course, the repressed is part of the unconscious, and I am sure Freud would not disagree that the psychoanalyst also represses some of what he hears, but most of the time the analyst is taking in the material, sorting it according to the patterns of serial logic, and thus hearing the logic of the unconscious.

VB: In your books you state that the receptive unconscious is the work of the ego.

CB: Yes. Although Freud used the word ego in many ways I have made it clear that I have adopted his use to signify the unconscious operation of the mind, or the intelligence of form. Although Freud does indeed recognize this ego—the part of the psyche that operates the theatre of conflict, or the container that holds the contents—he confuses matters by having the ego as part of a tripartite agency along with the Id and the Superego.

So we can fairly ask, well, what agency, what processional intelligence, would integrate those three domains? In my view it could only ever be the ego. The same is true of the topographic model. We have consciousness, the preconscious, and the unconscious. But what intelligence processes repression, collection in the unconscious, and the displaced return to consciousness? In his essay "The unconscious" (1915e), Freud haphazardly assigns the organizing function of the total system to the system preconscious: "it devolves upon the system Pcs. to make communication possible between the different ideational contents so that they can influence one another" (*ibid.*, p. 188) and he also assigns to the preconscious the function of time, reality testing, and the organization of conscious memory.

Here he burdens a concept to the point of meaninglessness. "It devolves upon the preconscious" by default. The preconscious is an important idea in the theory of repression because it operates as a form of "no" on the border between unconscious and conscious. It is a "no" that is informed by something unacceptable to consciousness for many reasons. It would, however, have to be part of the unconscious and not part of consciousness. It is a "no" heard by the self's unconscious, or, more accurately, anticipated by the self's unconscious given the self's psychic history, lived experience, and contextual existence. It is a "no" that demands creative unconscious work—for that is what occurs in displacement—and displacement is simply one of the ways in which we think unconsciously. The preconscious is a "no" derived from the unconscious and is subcontracted by the unconscious to return the forbidden ideas back into consciousness in some acceptable form.

VB: Where do you put Freud's theory of repression in your metaphor of the unconscious as symphony?

CB: The repressed erupts in language through the usual suspects of parapraxes. But, in fact, this accounts for a very small amount of unconscious representation in the course of an analysis. If the analyst does not see that at the same time there is another form of unconscious representation in narrative— the logic of sequence—then the majority of unconscious thought is missed. The image of a symphonic score allows us to imaginatively graph the horizontal—the sequential— movement of unconscious forms of thought. The vertical axis, which permits us to include the many differing forms of unconscious thinking, identifies the different types of unconscious systems of representation that exist simultaneously.

VB: So your model is an attempt to conceptually embrace the complexity of the unconscious.

CB: Yes. Think of the work that goes into composing a novel, a symphony, or a painting. Unconscious creativity of any depth is exceedingly complex. The idea that it is somehow mediated through the doors of the preconscious is an absurdity. Consider the act of listening to a symphony. Do we really believe we can conceptualize—that is "see" this—through the topographic model of perception?

VB: You divide the unconscious into different categories of articulation. I presume that this is an important part of your drawing our attention to how complex unconscious thinking actually is?

CB: Yes. Returning to Ryle's incredibly important point, we could examine a literary text according to the grammatical rules, the stylistic canons, and the logical rules. Each of these perspectives would look at the same material and view it differently and come to differing conclusions. They are not in contradiction with one another because they operate according to differing principles. This humble point is very important when undertaking consideration of something as vastly complex as a psychoanalytical session. We can look at it from many differing principles, or, as I am suggesting, orders, each of which is a different type of thinking. There are hundreds of different orders and they may all be classified under the realm of categories.

If we allow that one category is language, we note immediately the numerous orders under which any text—but now I must make it clear that I refer to the oddity of the psychoanalytical session, a text that includes the analyst—can be examined are as numerous as there are schools of thought and schools of thought yet to arrive.

So, language. The grammars of English or French or any language are pre-existent structures that determine the possibilities of our syntactical utterances. Obviously, from what I have been saying, I do not think the Lacanians are correct that the unconscious is structured like a language—language is only one form of unconscious thinking. To go back to the orchestral score metaphor, each of the categories on the vertical axis would have many orders, or respectively different idioms of articulation. *How* we say something is clearly important. The category, language, includes syntax, rhetorical strategies, illocutionary acts, and narrative logics of sequence amongst other orders. It cannot include the *sound* of the person's voice uttering these signifiers, although we should reserve the phonemic quality of a word under the category of language, rather than as an order under the domain of the sonic.

These two categories—language and the sonic, although separate, will be very close to one another, no more so, perhaps, than when regarding the phonemic sound of a word *and* the way a patient voices it. The sonic category would have to have an order, "voice", for the specific sound of the speaker's utterances. There are other auditory orders within this category, such as sounds emitted by body movement.

Returning to the sound of voice, we could construct a list of vocal signifiers such as sarcasm, despair, resignation, expectation, and so forth. In other words we are left now to find some way to represent *mental qualities or states of mind*.

VB: Are you referring to a form of index?

CB: Yes, an index that we could use to note the meaning of a word determined by its categorical context. For example, a person may express through the sound of voice or facial gesture the same mental states and we could use "d" to designate despair, "a" for anxiety, "j" for joy.

VB: How does this work with voice?

CB: Each speaker stresses certain words or syllables. As part of the speakers *sonic dynamic* we could establish a system of notation that certainly owes much to musical notation. We could use "*p*" for piano, "*pp*" for pianissimo, "*f*" for forte, and so forth.

VB: Are you saying that a session *could* be notated in this manner?

CB: In the same way that some musical notes are preceded by a notation such as "*pp*" to indicate the dynamic, so, too, we *could* (I do not say should) note words to help us perceive the mental dynamics of an hour. I do not propose that we do this as a matter of clinical practice. It is a heuristic device that permits us to appreciate how speakers unconsciously shape a session. We cannot possibly perceive this entirety consciously. Certain sonic emphases will, however, be dynamically significant enough to strike us. Setting aside for the moment a person's character speech (that is the signature of their voice) all individuals articulate unconscious meanings along these lines.

VB: You seem to be searching for ways to identify unconscious forms of thought.

CB: Yes, let us continue to think about the human voice and vocal dynamics.

Take *stress*. It may seem deceptively simple, but the stress we place on words in a phrase tells us something other than what is conveyed by the definition of the word.

Or consider *pitch*. This refers to how high or low a person speaks and although it is a close relative to stress it is measurable on an absolute scale as all sound has a precise pitch. All people have characteristic pitches according to the scale of their own voice. So, in addition to laying stress upon a particular word, they may simultaneously give this word a certain pitch. Given that pitch is the frequency on which a sound is uttered and that frequency is measured according to the vibrations per second, pitch is a form of psychosomatic communication. The speaker's vibration directly affects the listener's ear thereby tuning the other into the speaker's vibes.

Take *duration*. The intervals between words also become part of the enunciation. More generally, our unconscious is instructed by an analysand's *beat*. In the same way that in music time is measured according to beats (e.g., three beats to a measure), time, as a logic of sequence, moves according to the beat of a session. A person, for example, could speak very quickly so that his beat would be five to a measure, whereas another person would speak slowly and the beat would be one to a measure. Measures are grouped according to two types of beat: a strong and a weaker beat. Measures are also characterized by how many beats occur, and they come in twos or multiples of two, or in threes or multiples of three, and these then constitute meter. A person's *metrical character* will articulate his unconscious timing, something that is very hard to identify, even if it is an important part of both the act of communication and the recipient act of listening. More commonly, and also more complexly, however, a person will change his tempo in sessions according to differing states of mind.

Then there is *timbre*, which is the tonal quality of a speaker's voice. This is a subtle difference but it refers to the different qualities of say a piano or a violin. People have different timbres to their voice. They will also vary their tone colours according to the subject matter on their mind.

If we take all of the above together—stress, pitch, beat, timbre, duration—we have some of the ingredients of *vocal texture*. In musical language this would refer to the density of a work. Clearly, if many different notes are being played all with different timbres, if the metres vary and so forth, we have a dense articulation. In psychoanalysis it is not difficult to state whether one is with a patient who is speaking a dense texture or not. Silence, too, may be thick with meaning, even if it is not manifestly evident. A silence between thick verbal textures may well be in accord with the overall composition. If there is a perceivable falling off in density it is quite possible this is an indication of a resistance to what is being thought, or it may be an indication of a decathexis of a particular line of thought. It may herald a period of transitional silence as the patient leaves off one idea because another is arriving.

VB: How do you represent pitch, timbre, and so forth on your model of a score? Are they separate categories and if so would they have their own formal space on the vertical line?

CB: They are part of the sonic category. We could use the ordinary notations found in musical language, but I make this point only to illustrate something not to suggest that we put such a system into practice.

VB: The examples you have given of texture have been vocal.

CB: We can add non-vocal attributes that also articulate unconscious ideas. Take *colour*. In music it refers to timbre, although it can also refer to a particular type of orchestral idiom such as can be found in Debussy. We also refer to colour in language, to colourful phrasing. I can say, "Today I must go shopping", but that is not colourful. I could say, "Today I must go shopping for food"; that adds colour. I could say, "Today I will go to the market and look for some meat and fish", which gives more colour to the utterance. But if I were to say, "Today I shall go to Mr Steele's, on Flask Walk, to see if I can find some lamb shanks and then I will go to the Hampstead Fish Market to see if I can find some wild Norwegian salmon", the listener will have experienced a more colourful and specific utterance than those preceding it.

The colour of people's language varies. One of the most consistent problems found in the work of the analyst is that he or she accepts abstract language where a simple question would evoke more colourful phrases from the patient. A patient might say, "So yesterday I visited a few people", and the analyst might simply accept this as is and work with the concept of "visiting" and the people would be irrelevant. If the analyst echoed the last words and said, "People?", the analysand might then go on to say something like, "Yes, I saw my former husband who was in hospital and wanted to see me and when I was there I saw my former mother- and father-in-law, which was strange, and then later in the day I hung out with my editor, who had rather disturbing things to say about my latest novel." This description is far more specific and evocative than "I visited a few people."

Facilitation of lines of thought is a crucial function of the analyst's action potential. By stressing certain of the analysand's words or phrases the analyst asks the unconscious for help. It indicates that the analyst's unconscious is receptive to the smallest of details reported by the patient. For Freud, these seemingly "irrelevant details" were the most important.

Freud's injunction that patients be completely honest proved impossible. Ironically enough, analysands thought this meant they should talk about conscious matters that they preferred to keep secret. If Freud had been able to communicate to his analysands that he just wanted them to talk about their everyday life and not try to come up with deep dark secrets, he would have advanced the cause of free association enormously. It is in the links between seemingly trivial details of ordinary life, moving from one story to another, that the analysand reveals an unconscious logic that proves in time to be illuminating.

VB: I would like to come back to that point—your belief in the analysand's unconscious creativity—but for now I want to point to how your example illustrates the function of "voice". In effect, it seems as if this introduces the rhetoric of speech into the unconscious as a dynamic factor.

CB: Because enunciation is unconscious expression. We carry many ideas through the way we sound language. Our affects and emotional experiences are to a very large extent expressed through voice.

VB: Indeed, at this point it seems as if your symphony metaphor becomes even more pertinent.

CB: Yes and no. I use the image of the symphonic score because we know what it looks like and what it indicates. So it is useful as a model. And when we think of points of convergence, of how very different lines of thought meet at nodal points, then the sonic *realization* of the score is a relevant example as this is indeed how orchestral logic "speaks".

I do not intend for us to think of the unconscious as a symphony. It is a way of imagining it. It helps me to think of the dynamic of vertical and horizontal axes of unconscious thinking. I "see" Freud's model of the unconscious as a sequential logic of zig-zagging lines. *If* we connected the notes on a staff, then we would follow a musical line of thought as it moved both vertically and horizontally (or, in another words, diagonally). Hence the zig-zag. But a symphony will contain many differing lines of thought simultaneously, so if we wished to see the connection of those notes we would use a kind of colour code system illustrating how the lines moved in a pattern as they were played by differing instruments. As instruments of an orchestra serve in my model as categories of articulation, you can see how this metaphor allows us, from my point of view, to "see" separate lines of thought coming together (a nodal point), before following their respectively different paths.

VB: Can you say more about silence?

CB: The symphonic metaphor allows us to include silence as an active unconscious factor in our considerations. Sections of an orchestra may remain silent but we feel this silence. We can still hear themes played by, say, the violins or the French horns, even if these sections are orchestrally silent. Silence is present absence. Sometimes silence in an orchestral section may be more present by its absence of sonic contribution than those sections that are sonically active.

Bruckner had this down to an art. Who can listen to the Ninth symphony without having the horn section almost always in mind, especially in the quiet sections, which we know will be torn up by the rupturing sound of the horns? When they arrive it is usually temporally expected. We appreciate how *this* unconscious logic—musical thinking—carries us through memory to a form of desire, as previously played melodies, once re-stated, bring expectations for similar pattern completions. Bruckner both will and will not fulfil that desire. Silence plays a crucial role in the emotions of expectation, frustration, delay, and gratification.

In music, there is also a form of sound termed "silounds", which refers to the other sounds that one can hear when the composer creates silence. These might be the sounds of people moving about in the audience or of someone coughing. In an analytical session silence may allow for the silounds of the two participants' breathings, or the sound of the stomachs gurgling. Those silences move both outward and inward at the same time. Outward, as these silences open the session out to the sounds surrounding the analytical couple that are not part of the deep texture of speech, but they move inward because attention is drawn to the soma and to the soma as a category of unconscious articulation.

The most obvious such occasion would be a silence that permits the analyst to perceive a form of distress occurring in the analysand, a kind of deep breathing indicating unspeakable anguish, perhaps accompanied by tears but not the sound of crying.

In addition, silence permits one to hear what music theorists refer to as "biomusic", the sound of the non-human (even if animal) sound-world surrounding the participants. These might be the sounds of a dog barking, a postman putting letters through a letterbox, the sound of a phone ringing in the distance, the sound of the wind, the sound of the door shutting in the waiting room. An analysand may be silent in order

to speak something through the biomusic, even if this is acci-
dental music, so to speak. But allowing the sounds of the
outside world to speak within a session has unconscious
significance and is part of the subset of the order of silence.

VB: So we have basic categories of expression in a psychoanalytic
session and we have lines of thought operating within their
own orders as part of a category.

CB: Categories are generic forms of thinking and articulating
unconscious ideas. A line of thought can use different orders
simultaneously or move through forms, such as when a logical sequence of narrative thought is also expressed by tone of
voice and by silence. These other lines of thought express
thinking through those respectively different categories.

So let us imagine that a patient says "I FIND my uncle
INTERESTING." This is part of a narrative and follows the
analysand's telling of her need for guidance, of her appreciation for analysis. The session begins by her saying that she
thinks she is missing a lover in her life but does not find
men interesting enough. So we can see that quite possibly
the narrative sequence leads to the uncle–analyst as an object
of desire. Stress is placed on the word "find" so that it draws
attention to the uncle as a found object. The pitch of the
voice deepens and simultaneously is accompanied by a rich
timbre that gives a kind of sultry emphasis to "find". She
pauses after saying find, and also pauses after saying "my
uncle", so her beat says the following: "I . . . FIND . . . my uncle
. . . INTERESTING." Duration and syntax here combine to isolate
and emphasize the subject, the object, and the adverbial
qualities of the patient's thinking. At the same time, the
patient rolls over on her side, curls up, and puts her hand
under her head. The body speaks. The analyst feels this as
erotic, so the order of countertransference joins the other
orders and categories. A line of thought expresses itself
through several different categories at the same time, for just
a few seconds.

VB: Some of these orders are, of course, unique to psychoanalysis.

CB: Yes, absolutely. While the orders under the category of language or the sonic will be familiar to people in other discip-
lines, the order of transference—understood as a form of

unconscious thinking—is appreciated only by psychoanalysis. If we add countertransference we see how this instrument of unconscious articulation is even more specific to psycho-analysis, as it is only the psychoanalyst who understands that what goes on within himself or herself is *often* the patient's articulation of an idea that can only be thought through the other's inner experience.

VB: So the symphony metaphor is even more apt, is it, because musical ideas express themselves through different instru-ments? A theme can be sounded by the horns, the timpani, and the violins, each with differing sounds, each with its own pitch, texture, and vibrant duration.

CB: Yes, it is one of the reasons why it is useful as it allows us to imagine unconscious processes. It has concept-potential.

VB: How do we distinguish between categories and lines of thought?

CB: Categories refer to fundamentally different forms of articulate thought. Writing out a word, speaking it, dancing an idea, enacting it in a relationship, follow different form character-istcs. The same idea, however, can be thought—or expressed—in different categories at the same time.

Imagine the statement "I want to go to the barn to fetch a pail of water". As a logic of narrative sequence this may be part of a train of thought that reveals the unconscious idea "I have been searching for good milk but can't find any, even in a barn, so I will have to make do with water". At the same time, however, it is accompanied by a brusque wave of the hand. The body speaks. Alone, without wording, the gesture would be hard to follow. Accompanying the wording it may express the idea of brusque oscillation that expresses the variant between milk and water.

Let us include voice. The speaker stresses the word "want" but hits the word "water" with a tone of disappointment. This articulation expresses the idea of wanting and the idea of being disappointed through the sounding of the sentence. The word "want" is part of a phonemic chain of ideas in the session, the patient having used other words that sound like it: "I go wanting"; "wait"; "wandering". The sounds seem to say that the self is wandering about in a wanting state of mind.

Add the orders of the transference and countertransference, part of the relational category. The illocutionary impact of the sentence within transference thinking is a demand for analytical gratification. The analyst, besieged by endless wantings in this patient, feels "oh no, not again, this person is always wanting". We could go on, but I think this is enough to make a point. We see a line of thought expressed simultaneously in different categories of unconscious articulation, the total effect is not unlike that of a musical idea expressed through the harmonization of differing instruments.

VB: Is this one line, then, or many lines of thought?

CB: It is a line of thought expressed through different categories and their orders at the same time. When Freud posited his theory of nodal points, he argued that different lines of thought can join along the same path for a while before going separate ways. Here we see a single sentence, expressed in differing categories at the same time. Drives, memories, object relational paradigms, and other psychic phenomena will be articulated in different orders. They do not always "speak" in one order alone. A drive may be expressed in language, or in the pulsion of speaker's voice, or in a body movement, or in the psychoanalyst's countertransference.

VB: How does the dream work conceptualize these forms of unconscious thinking? If we stick to condensation, displacement, substitution, and so forth, how do we see it at work in this particular category?

CB: Harmonization is condensation. An idea may be expressed in different categories (or different orders within the same category) that converge in a harmonic sense as they are all of a piece. But each separate articulation can be isolated and discovered of its own accord. In turn, those articulations may be developing themes within their own life-line that precede the given harmonic moment that relates to other harmonies and melodies.

We can also refer to musical thinking when conceptualizing simultaneous but separate lines of thought that do not converge but play off one another, such as occurs in polyphony or counterpoint. In polyphony there are separate lines of thought that go together but pursue their own melodies.

Again, I am not suggesting that the unconscious is structured like music because I do not think it is. But the elements of music and the musical score do give us as good a representation of the dynamic movement of unconscious life as any other model we may find. As music is a form of unconscious thinking—albeit just one form—it none the less illustrates the unconscious in ways that painting and even writing cannot accomplish. For example, it is only in music that one can articulate (and perceive) separate ideas expressed simultaneously. Music merges separate elements into temporary harmonic melodies. It can also assemble the ideational, the affective, and the bodily in ways not organizable through other unconscious forms of articulation. It gets inside one and yet it is outside one. Listening to music one is awake, yet inside a dream logic of the other's creation. I think this is also true of the analyst's subjective status in the psychoanalytical experience.

If we submit to unconscious communications then we will be carried off by the many different systems of unconscious expression like those one finds in listening to music. Indeed, each of the major forms of artistic expression—music, fiction, painting—derives from its own unconscious process. Obviously, they are not the same. Thankfully, I do not have to take up that issue and only refer to the musical score as an image psychoanalysts may employ as a scaffold upon which they can construct a theory of unconscious articulation in the clinical hour.

VB: You think we can learn how to understand the unconscious better than we do?

CB: If we understand that unconscious forms of articulation are sequential, and if we are trained to follow these sequences, then our receptive unconscious builds perceptual matrices for the comprehension of such sequences. If we resist the understanding of sequences; if, for example, we foreclose unconscious articulation through premature organization of material, then we will not learn to read the unconscious.

VB: Well then, let's think of something else. How about rhythm? Is this part of sequential thinking?

CB: There are characteristic rhythms to a person's session. A way of beginning, a set of pauses, of hesitations, of sudden significant remarks, divergences, returns to a main theme if briefly, then what seem to be splittings off when the analyst may feel the patient has wandered off entirely from the unconscious main themes, but then—again as with music—a return to the main theme. The analyst's unconscious will not only perceive that rhythm, he will attune to it. He will get into the rhythm unless it is so a-rythmic and discordant that this asserts itself as a manifestation of a character problem. Apatient may have no rhythm other than a constant theme, with no variation, no texture, nothing. That certainly brings itself to the analyst's attention.

VB: What about moods?

CB: Musical works are usually in a certain key. C-Major is typically a key of joy and jubilation, C-Minor of concentration and introspection, A-Flat Major of celebration and human devotion. In the same way we have moods. It would be helpful in a clinical presentation to be informed of the mood of the session. It is the tone in which an individual expresses the self.

VB: In the Baroque period there was an attempt to make a direct link between music and the emotions.

CB: The Doctrine of Affects. Well, this is understandably seen as an antiquated effort, in part because they incorrectly thought that there could be a direct correspondence between a musical note and an emotion. So a major key that moved quickly was the equivalent of a happy state of mind. Music certainly does play upon our affects. It constructs emotional experiences that are themselves predicated on the major key of the work. But when we articulate unconscious affects or emotions or mental qualities a sequence of any such expression owes its meaning not to some external criteria (fast means happy) but to the internal psychic logic of the subject who speaks.

VB: How do you understand mental qualities?

CB: It is fine for us to identify certain major affects such as anxiety or depression, but I think these are very crude categories that tell us very little about a person's state of mind. An emotion is not self defining because, although it will be composed of certain affects, it is also composed of ideas and other psychical matters. There are, however, identifiable qualities to the way we articulate unconscious ideas that are neither as crude as affects or as complex as emotions.

Let's take "irony" for example. Is this an affect? It certainly is not affectless *per se*. But it is a lot more than an affect. We know that it is faked ignorance that is intended to provoke an other. It is in part a speech act that infers the opposite of what is literally said. It may be conveyed, in part, by a subtle tone of sarcasm so we can see how voice enters the picture. But it need not use voice. One could say to the other "you certainly do know what you are talking about" and roll one's eyes up to the sky so that one's face renders this an ironic comment.

Take the quality of "effort." Again is that an affect? Yes and no. I think it is more a frame of mind composed of many elements. So, too, with many other mental qualities: curiosity, enthusiasm, earnestness, thoughtfulness, numbness, bewilderment, seductiveness, despair, and so on. We could use an index to identify these mental qualities. We can see that notation of these mental qualities is entirely dependent on our ability to perceive them. Irony may be lost because some "do not get it". An index of mental qualities, then, allows us to identify and notate a subtle "language" that is unconsciously acquired, entirely dependent on our psychic maturities, and deeply significant to ourselves as conscious beings. A feeling is, as we know, a transitional state of mind between unconscious perceptions and conscious registrations of what is being perceived as it happens. Part of that perceptual act is the perception of these qualities.

VB: So if we were writing up a clinical presentation you would want to see some system of notation that would indicate the mental qualities of discourse?

CB: Only if we were engaged in a study of unconscious communication. It helps to illuminate the dynamic complexity of the mind.

VB: One critique of your symphonic model is that it seems to eliminate the analytical concept of conflict. What is psychodynamic about it? How do the forces interact in this model if everything is rather moving along, all as a kind of ensemble?

CB: The conflicts of the mind are deployed unconsciously. We think them unconsciously. It is important to distinguish between unconscious conflicts and the unconscious that organizes these conflicts. The symphonic model is a way of conceptualizing how the unconscious works.

In the movement of this symphony many differing lines of thought may be in conflict with one another. So, if one is following an idea in the flow of free associations, it may give rise to an opposition through voice or through transference (i.e., acting upon). It is helpful to bear in mind that this model addresses the fact that as we think unconsciously most of the time, we are thus thinking our conflicts unconsciously and that such thinkings will, of course, include the oppositions in the mind as they are thought.

VB: And defences?

CB: Defences are mental actions that may be articulated in many different ways, from a statement within the logic of narrative sequence that expresses denial, or reversal into the opposite, or a reaction formation, to the category of the imaginary and, in particular, the order of projection where parts of the self are expressed through splits assembled in different objects, to isolations of affect expressed through the sound of voice.

VB: Is the idea that we are absorbed in many different lines of thought one of the reasons why you specify that we not be so absorbed in the transference?

CB: One of the reasons, yes. While transference is an order that takes place *all* the time, the fact that *it is there* does not mean that it subsumes into itself all the other orders and their categories of unconscious thinking. As discussed, Freud never envisioned the transference in this way. The transference could be "unobjectionable", which means that nothing of unconscious significance was operating there. The patient might be using the analyst's mind to assist his own unconscious process of thought. This is use of the object. Transference is a *form* of thinking. If we assume that transference is an acting upon the analyst, it can be a useful acting upon (as in collaboration), it can be an invasive deposition of unwanted parts of the personality, it can be an acting of the father upon the analyst now cast in the position of the analysand's child self. There are simply too many types of actings-upon to enumerate them. But all of them are part of the order of transference that is part of the relational category.

VB: How do you envision projection as a form of articulation? Is it in the relational category? As in "object relations"?

CB: I think we have to divide the imaginary world and the relational world into two separate categories. Otherwise, a term such as projection is so saturated that it loses its meaning. At this point I would suggest a category, the imaginary (after Lacan), that includes projection as one of its orders. This would refer to projection as it takes place in the "internal world", which to be sure is a relational universe, but within the category of the imaginary.

This recognizes something we all know, that we not only think in images, but we also paint them, or draw them, or sculpt them, so clearly there is a very different form for articulation of unconscious ideas operating in this category. And, while there is a long-standing debate over whether images can be conveyed in words—some would argue they are always subordinate to language and never conveyed in-themselves— I do think that in so far as psychoanalysis is concerned we recognize that analysands portray their internal world. At times we think in pictures and when we speak them, even though they are immediately subjected to the category of language, wording is none the less able to transfer the imaginary into its own articulated realm. We can imagine along with the speaker, thinking in pictures.

I suggest the relational category embrace projective identification, which I would now use to define those forms of projection that use actual objects or others to carry parts of the self. Included in the relational category are, of course, the transference, but as an enactment, as something in which the analyst is acted upon. Returning to the imaginary category, we would also find another order for the transference, so, confusing though this may be, we would have two different orders marked transference. But the transference that takes place in the imaginary category is so different from the transference that takes place in the relational category that I believe this intrinsic difference necessitates conceptual recognition. The relational category embraces a field of actual relations between self and the object world, most notably with others, that also includes an order of inter-relating, an order of subject relations, and the other orders we have discussed. Time does not permit us to discuss this further, but I hope in the future to return to this topic.

VB: Back to conscious reasoning. You are arguing that our consciousness is unconsciously determined, even including what we think of as reasoned thought?

CB: Yes. Here now, however, we are in another region, that of unconscious perception. We have thus far been discussing unconscious articulation. Each of the orders of expression is also receptive. As discussed elsewhere, the unconscious mind not only grows, it is constituted out of its growth. As we think through different categories (and their orders) we not only articulate our thoughts in more diverse and complex ways, we simultaneously expand our unconscious perceptive capabilities.

VB: To return to unconscious thinking, you argue that much if not all of the work of a psychoanalysis is unconscious. You refer to Freud's theory of evenly suspended attentiveness. Would you comment further?

CB: I think the only reason why this seems a difficult issue is because of the confusion of the two theories of the unconscious in analysis. If you pick the Freud who saw the unconscious as primitive and instinct driven, if you then link this as did he to the Id and see the unconscious as aboriginal, it is hard then to switch frames of reference to appreciate how sophisticated unconscious forms of thought are. But when Freud said that he grasped the drift of the patient's unconscious with his own unconscious, he implicitly recognized the intelligence of unconscious processes. The unconscious here was certainly not the system unconscious of his topographic model or the Id of his structural model.

VB: You obviously think this has widespread clinical implications.

CB: If I had to pick one area in which I think psychoanalysis suffers from a devastating blindness it is here, in the failure to comprehend the unconscious creativity of the analysand. This is a tragedy not only for the clinician, who loses sight of the contributions of the analysand, but, more importantly, it means that analysands have suffered throughout generations of psychoanalysis. We have lost sight of how the analysand works within psychoanalysis. Such work was not dependent on analysis to begin with; indeed, psychoanalysis evolved out of a recognition of this work. The psychoanalyst became a working partner with the way we all think. Freud's appreciation of the logic of sequence tacitly celebrates the cooperation of the analysand, who cannot help but speak according to his or her unconscious. So, it is only a matter of time before the analyst's unconscious grasps a pattern of thought (doubtless from differing forms for unconscious thinking) that enables him or her to understand something.

VB: But what do you say to those analysts who, upon hearing this, would argue that you are leaving out how patients resist analysis or try to break the links in their own thoughts or for whom the defences are so intense that they have little insight into the self?

CB: We must first appreciate the presence of unconscious creativity and cooperation in the analysand before addressing resistances. Analysands are at work on multiple issues in their analysis. It is not the analyst who gets them to work on this. They are invested in working on psychic issues.

VB: What is the motivation?

CB: Pleasure.

VB: Pleasure?

CB: Mental pain, psychic confusion, or the "questionable" drives us to resolve its unpleasure. We work to understand something because understanding is, in the very first sense, pleasurable. It may eventually become pleasing because to understand is to fulfil a wish for meaning or, more simply, to master a difficult reality. We engage in unconscious work because we are driven to do so by the pleasure principle that finds in "combinatory play" the pleasure of thinking. So, thinking is ultimately in the service of the pleasure principle.

VB: I sense an "and".

CB: Thinking is also necessary to survival. Our species would not have survived without unconscious processes of thought. So we are also at work on issues that trouble us—and could endanger us in the phylogenetic sense—by seeking out solutions to the problem. Thus, the reality principle is a part of the reason why we strive to solve problems in analysis, but not in the narrow sense of the analysand seeking to solve a particular problem because he or she thinks they should. It precedes such an urge. Even if the person was consciously avoidant and did not want to attend to the issues they presented, they would not be able to stop the part of the personality that strives to solve these issue as we are driven to do so.

VB: How does this observation fit into your way of working?

CB: I think it is an important part of the therapeutic alliance for the analyst to point out to the analysand how he or she is creating the analysis. However important the analyst's role, it is ultimately dependent on what the patient creates. Most analysands are oblivious to their own creativity. By reflecting upon their many lines of thought we indicate to the analysand how rich a source of thinking he or she really is.

This is not a micro academic moment. By referring the analysis to the analysand's unconscious we support that object relation between consciousness and unconsciousness. This helps the analysand appreciate the practical reasons for the free associative process because then he or she can see why they are encouraged to simply speak whatever comes to mind. It also develops their appreciation of unconscious thinking itself.

Psycho-historically, this builds on an object relation that has been repressed or lost due to infantile amnesia: the self's relation to an intelligent other, embodied in the mother. The self's relation to the mother is, amongst other things, a relation to one's own unconscious, as in the beginning the foetal and the maternal unconscious are barely distinguishable. In time the effective presence of the maternal unconscious recedes as the self's unconscious emerges in its own right, although, of course, it will have assumed much that was conveyed by the maternal object.

Just as the maternal unconscious looked after us, so, too, does our unconscious, and I think we know this. Our sense that we should trust our "gut instincts" or "sense" of things means that we give ourselves over to our unconscious sense of things rather than to some other order. This does not mean we are right. Indeed, our gut response may be quite wrong. But the object relation is important.

Psychoanalytic work, as it takes place between consciousness and the unconscious, renews the self's deep relation to
the maternal logic, and I think this is part of the progressive
evolution of a self.

VB: Even if it involves what would appear to be a regression?

CB: Being linked again to the maternal order through the Freudian
Pair lifts the repression of this order and avails a self of a
deeper level of creativity than would otherwise be the case.

VB: And how does this link to practice?

CB: The analysand, when first confronted by the analyst's attention to the order of his or her thinking, is likely to view this
with a form of contempt. That contempt towards the self's
own unconscious is a complex matter, but a feature of it is the
contempt towards the maternal order. By returning the self to
a generative object relation between self and maternal order
we liberate this order within us, we allow it to become a vital
part of the way we live. We also give a proper status to maternal order evidence.

The chain of ideas revealed through the logic of sequence is
now put into a proper place. However much is said about
how subjective or intersubjective the analytical process is—
i.e., as in lacking in objectivity—it is certainly not true of the
order of sequence. The order of the presentation of thoughts
is an *oral text* and constitutes the integrity of the analysand's
evidence in the clinical hour.

Whatever the analyst may think or feel about this, however
he may forget aspects of it or change parts of it, doing so is
irrelevant to the integrity of that text. The failure to appreciate
this oral text, however, or to subjugate it to the analyst's own
presumed "co-constructive" licence is simply to symptoma-
tize the continued denigration of unconscious life.

VB: I want to turn to another line of articulation, to syntax. How
does a grammatical pattern express unconscious processes of
thought and, further, how does this fit into your model of
the symphony, as syntactical patterns are part of discourse
analysis and not ordinarily thought of as part of musical
language?

CB: We speak in syntactical patterns. This is observed by scruti-
nizing a writer's ways of forming sentences. Such syntactical

patterns constitute an independent line of unconscious thinking. The correspondent in music would be the typical ways of forming musical phrases, employing the grammar of music.

While a logic of narrative sequence is discoverable because we can recall the manifest contents and ultimately, in some cases, discover the latent links, the syntax as unconscious expression is almost completely outside of consciousness within an analysis. This refers to a person's style as a speaker and, although it can be studied linguistically, the effect on the analyst is part of the analysand's rhetoric.

VB: And character?

CB: Character is a line of articulation, part of the relational category. As discussed, however, any line can express its logic through multiple categories, and this is certainly true of character, as it will be articulated through all the different categories we have identified. When we express ourselves to an other we do so within all the categories we have discussed. The horizontal movement of a self's character would constitute simultaneous actions in these categories, following a highly idiomatic pattern.

VB: So character exists, then, only in the eyes of the beholder?

CB: The other is instrumental to the perception of character. I cannot perceive my own character but I convey it to the other, who experiences it. In this respect such experience is perception.

VB: How would you define that perception?

CB: The other's receptive unconscious perceives any pattern. Character is a pattern. We learn about this type of pattern, just as we learn about the idioms of language, music, and gesture, from experience. By the time we are young adults we are actually quite skilled in character perception, and it plays a big role in why we are attracted to some people and not to others. In very intimate relations there is a deep mutual character perception taking place.

VB: And in analysis?

CB: The analyst does experience the analysand's character. Because the analyst is neutral—he has neutralized his character up to a point—he opens himself to a deep reception of the other's impact upon himself: to *otherness*. Through the many hours of being *impressed* by that character, its idiom establishes itself in the analyst's unconscious as a matrix of thing presentations.

VB: I want to return us to the crux of this discussion, your use of the symphonic score as a model of the unconscious. Some will think that you believe the unconscious works in the same way as musical thought, especially as you have drawn upon some of the features of musical composition—beat, timbre, etc.—to illuminate different categories of unconscious articulation.

CB: The point of this model is to give us a working image of Freud's theory of free association.

The horizontal axis pictures sequence. For Freud, it was the logic of sequence that revealed latent mental contents, and the musical score allows us to visualize this.

The vertical axis allows us to imagine the different categories of the sequential. It addresses the question "what is being sequenced?"

A category is also a separate way of thinking. And certainly if we take the order, narrative sequence—the serial logic that fascinated Freud—we follow Freud's exact meaning of the logic of sequence. He attends to what we learn from the inherent logic in the chain of ideas. The logic is not implicit in the separate units of narrative manifest content. It is to be found in the latent connective "tissue" that *itself* only becomes clear in time when a logic connecting all the separate manifest contents reveals itself. The latent contents can only be retrospectively grasped, at least consciously.

On the other hand, unconsciously, the analyst's receptive unconscious, which looks for and organizes everything into patterns, is discovering patterns in the connective tissues of thought and often the pattern of thought arrives in the analyst's consciousness as an inspired idea.

It is not dissimilar to anyone's pleasure at finding a pattern. I have added other orders, however, because, although narrative sequence is a most important way of thinking, it is not the only one. Moreover, lines of thought moving within other categories converge in nodal points that for some time join different categories together in the simultaneous expression of thought.

Perhaps I should point out a way in which I expand Freud's model of line of thought. For Freud, the nodal point is a convergence of unconscious lines of thought where they join together for a while and then disperse. The dream is the exemplar of a nodal point as it is a convergence of many lines of thought into one object, after which they go separate ways. But a line of narrative thought expressed in a session may be significant as a logic of narrative progression.

Meaning is resident in the unfolding logic of sequence, yet at the same time the objects presented through the manifest content (the story and its characters) may indicate another line of thought that we would understand as projective.

Now which do you choose? Is one right and the other wrong? Add to this the emotional significance of the narrative line of thought. Add further the metrical structure or the illocutionary force of the utterance. Do we ignore these orders of articulation?

We cannot, it seems to me. Each category is registered by our receptive unconscious which chooses an order within a category depending on which one *seems* to take priority over the others, usually because several categories of thinking join together in articulating the idea. Or, the category picks the analyst!

VB: That seems crucial. You are saying that we focus consciously on any line of thought emerging from a category (or categories) based on its coming into the foreground of consciousness.

CB: Yes. It may be that *I am made aware* through the category of transference that the analysand's references are to myself, but the order, of narrative sequence, seems to me a more compelling line of thought. It is not to dismiss the transference line, but only to indicate that in that moment the narrative sequence is the more significant.

VB: How is it possible to listen to the material in both the Freudian and in the Kleinian manner? The Freudian reception seems predicated on a form of listening that does not interpret the discourse as object relational, while the Kleinian or British approach understands the people or events as always carrying projected parts of the analysand or representations of other objects. How can you listen to the material from these two very different perspectives?

CB: Your unconscious decides. If you believe as I do that listening to the material from both perspectives is a legitimate way of perceiving psychic reality, then you leave it up to the analysand's unconscious and your unconscious to decide which of the two is the more forceful category in determining your attention cathexes.

VB: At the beginning of the hour, however, how are you disposed?

CB: I am relaxed. While I understand what analysts mean by being terrified of their patients or in a state of on-the-edge-of-the-seat anxiety, this is not how I begin an hour. I am in something of a meditative state. I have no demand on myself to listen out for anything and I have no expectation that I will say something meaningful. In that way I follow Freud's construction of evenly suspended attentiveness very closely. An entire session or more may pass by with me in that frame of mind, saying next to nothing of significance because I have nothing to say.

It may be important to share this with the analysand so I do not leave him or her in the dark on this. In any event, I indicate early on in an analysis how I work and the analysand knows that I am not going to jump in to say something for the sake of creating meaning.

But in most sessions I do focus on something. Conscious recognition of a meaningful pattern is delightful, isn't it? If I am lucky it usually arrives from the category of narrative sequence, and I will attend to what the analysand seems to be working on.

VB: So we have all these categories. They move sequentially but not all are active at the same time. Indeed, silence is an order that presumably halts many of the other orders. Do you see unconscious articulation, then, as somehow integrated by these respective categories? Do they harmonize as they move along?

CB: No and yes. Freud's concept of the nodal moment addresses the occasion when several lines of thought converge into one representational correspondence. In that respect, using the musical score as a model to picture this process, we can say there is a harmonization of the lines of thought.

But otherwise, and in my view for the most part, unconscious lines of thought have little to do with one another. Indeed, lines of thought have separate temporalities. Some are unconsciously inactive for months, possibly years, the links few and far between, while other lines of thought occur daily. The history of a composer's work does allow one to perceive this variance, as some melodies have variations that occur frequently in a composer's work whereas there are other times when a theme occurs once and then not again for decades. Where has it been all those years? Where are the lines of thought that have not been represented in an analysand's discourse for months, if not years? They have always been there. They have always been active in the unconscious but they have not been articulated.

You will appreciate that thus far we have not discussed unconscious thought, only unconscious articulation. Freud went so far as to describe unconscious processes and certain characteristics, but no further. I think we have to leave it at that for the time being, and perhaps for a very long time indeed.

VB: We have covered quite a lot of ground in these discussions, which I appreciate are part of early considerations of these topics on your part.

CB: That is certainly true, but it is very important to point out that the model I am proposing is quite limited. Its main aim is to provide conceptual home to the differing forms of sequential logic inherent to the various orders of unconscious articulation.

I am, in particular, interested in the logic of narrative sequence that Freud proposed as his fundamental theory of unconscious expression, discoverable in the latent logic of the analysand's free associations. We have discussed other forms of sequential logic and their respective orders (and categories) because I think it is useful to contextualize narrative logic.

VB: Yet, you have clearly argued for a new way of thinking about the complexity of the unconscious and part of your tentative formulations include a system of classifying categories and orders of thinking that might help us to further analyse an analytical session.

CB: Yes, perhaps. But if we think of conceptualizing defences, for example, the model I use to imagine unconscious expression is less useful in thinking about defence than, say, the models provided by ego psychology and Kleinian conceptualization. Every model is limited and my own vision, so to speak, is no exception.

VB: At this point, what do you recommend to the reader?

CB: If the reader has grasped the point, if he gets the basic argument, then he should forget about it.

VB: You assume it will then be in the unconscious and serve its purpose?

CB: Yes.

CHAPTER THREE

Perceptive identification

Psychoanalysts are familiar by now with the theory of projective identification even if they do not agree with it. The aim of this brief essay is to propose another concept—perceptive identification—to make a distinction in object relations theory.

The term projective identification is often used to describe the projection of unwanted (not necessarily bad) parts of a personality either into an internal object or into an actual other, or both. It may be a way of evacuating and storing parts of a self—which serves many functions. The self may be denuded by off-loading such parts, but they can be contacted through forms of psychic remote-control.

The concept of projective identification is often used to explain how the self can identify empathically with the other. Think of Hamlet. We can become Hamlet mentally because—Oedipal creatures that we are—we project ourselves into his character.

A problem with this singular concept of identification, however, is that it runs the risk of assuming that Hamlet exists because we have created him through our projections. First, Hamlet has to exist before we can project ourselves into him.

Another problem is that although projective identification will always play *some* role in our relation to Hamlet, working exclusively from this theory of perception, identification, empathy, and critical appraisal risks destroying the integrity of the object itself. It is hard to escape the ironic realization that a theory meant to identify how we perceive the other by mental entry may result in the replacement of the other by the self.

Some time ago I proposed a developmental stage after the so-called "depressive position",[1] a period in the child's life when he or she appreciates "the integrity" of an object. I named this the era of "object integrity" and termed this ur-object the "integral object" (Bollas, 1995, pp. 87–92).

I think that Winnicott's theory of the "use of the object" describes a stage in the self's recognition of the integral object. By destroying the object through subjective use, the infant develops a particular love of the object because it survives his imaginative recreation of it. Next is appreciation of the object's qualities.

A problem with the concept of projective identification is that it is not categorically interested in the object's qualities *per se*, but in the self's projections into the object.

Perceptive identification is based on the self's ability to perceive the object as a thing-in-itself.[2] If the self can do this then it can enjoy the object's qualities and be nurtured by the integrity of the object. The more it can perceive the object-in-itself, the more it celebrates the object as different from the self. This model presupposes the *jouissance* of difference (not similarity) and implicitly appreciates the separateness of the object.

Perceptive identification allows us to love an object. A mature form of love, it does not function in accord with the intrinsically narcissistic axioms of projection and introjection. Psychoanalysis has long recognized these processes as mentally primitive.

Rather than separateness and difference leading to emotional distance—as some might assume—such love creates the possibility for a wider range and greater depth of intimacy with the object or other. By perceiving the object's features, the object is loved *for itself* not *for oneself*.

It is for specifically clinical reasons that I propose we use this term. In recent years I have been concerned by a surprisingly wide-spread disinterest on the part of therapists and analysts about what the analysand is actually saying. The crucial early words of a session, the unconscious selection of topics, the patterns of ideas that reveal themselves (eventually) through the movement from one topic to another, the ring of certain phrases, the evocative and ramifying effect of a single word, the far-reaching suggestion of a metaphor, are of so little interest to many clinicians that they are either not recalled or overlooked.

Freud defined "classical psychoanalysis" as the act of following the chain of ideas presented by the analysand (Freud, 1932a, p. 11). He acknowledged it was his least complex theory, perhaps because it was simply a way of saying that the analyst should listen to what the analysand says and to pay attention to the order of ideas.

Surprisingly few analysts can actually do this. Instead, under the aegis of the relational, the co-constructive, of "playing", or "a feeling", or "analysis of the transference", analysts jump into the session so early that it is not possible to perceive the analysand's free associations. (Given this *degree* of over intrusiveness it is not long before the analysand will stop free associating.)

In other words, there can be no perceptive identification if the analyst or therapist intervenes before the analysand is able to establish his narrative, affective, and character identity in the session. Such early interventions are the stuff of projective identification when the analyst feels he knows what is going on right away, or if not, assumes that knowing what he feels, or thinks, or . . . well, whatever! . . . is licence enough to say anything.

(It is important to keep in mind, however, that the respective categories of analysing the relationship, or taking into account the intersubjective, or the analyst's impact on the analysand, *are crucial*, but they are *separate* phenomenon. To merge them with the other categories—such as free association—is to commit a category error (Ryle, 1949). Imagine that a theatre critic has reviewed *Hamlet* but his newspaper receives a letter criticizing him for failing to describe the backstage production. This complaint is an example of a category error. Or, imagine that a literary critic has written about *Hamlet* as an exploration of sibling rivalries, but a reviewer takes the author to task for failing to discuss the syntactical structures of the play. That is another category error. Such errors constitute an intellectual pandemic in contemporary psychoanalytical discourse.)

Perceptive identification is predicated on the assumption that self and object are not the same and that the object's difference is vital to the self because of its separateness and distinctness. Although, in the realm of human relations, perceptive identification recognizes that self and other will at the same time share common human elements and psychic structures, the other's integrity is so unique that time must be given for any self to begin to perceive it.

In clinical work this knowledge recognizes the necessity of the analysand's establishment of his or her integrity within the hour, first through enough talk-time to reveal patterns *in* thought, second, to articulate some of the many different dimensions of character as *it is spoken*, third, to allow time for affects to become emotional experiences.

If projective identification gets inside the other, perceptive identification stands outside to perceive the other. The term "identification" means quite different things for each concept. In projective identification it means identifying with the object, in perceptive identification it means perceiving the identity of the object. Both forms of knowing need to work in tandem with one another in a creative oscillation between appreciating the integrity of the object and perceiving its identity, and then projecting parts of the self into the object, a form of imagination.

Think of poetry or fiction. However much we put ourselves into a text—distorting it, going off into reverie, putting our life into it— such liberty would only be evacuative if we did not perceive the work's integrity. Indeed, the theory of projection as evacuation is only possible if the integrity of the object is of no interest to the self, in which case any object will do as a psychic toilet.

Perceptive identification is not equivalent to "taking in" the object. Our use of the concept of introjective identification could err in the same way as seeing perceptive identification as a form of projection. It does not have to do with either putting something into or taking something from the object. It is a matter of seeing the qualities of the object.

A theory of perceptive identification may enable us to think differently about the complex way that we use objects. Perceptive, projective, and introjective identifications will overlap and often occur simultaneously. Perceptive identification, however, can occur only if one lingers long enough in the presence of the object or other for the love-base of this form of knowing to become effective.

Notes

1. See Eigen (2004) for an illuminating discussion of psychic life beyond the depressive position.
2. For a fine discussion of the self's appreciation of the qualities of an object, please see Schachtel, 1984, pp. 167–170.

CHAPTER FOUR

What is theory?

I

When Freud wrote himself into a corner he would engage a literary trope. It would go something like "if you believe what I have been arguing up till now you will have been following the wrong line of thought." Then off he would go on his merry way leaving many a reader flummoxed over why so much time had been spent thinking incorrect ideas. Freud's writing simply demonstrated his view that we think free associatively. Typically, he followed not just one line of thought but scores of "chains of ideas"—a term he often used, like "trains of thought". When these lines of thought were in outright contradiction with one another, Freud would engage the above trope or claim he was stuck and defer the issue until later.

I find a particular moment in *The Ego and the Id* (1923b) touching. Writing about the repressed unconscious, Freud is about to finish up Chapter One when a thought pops into his mind. Not only are the repressed contents unconscious but so, too, is the agency that commits them to the unconscious. He pauses. He states that it would seem that he has several different theories of the unconscious. For a moment he turns to God to see if the issue can be resolved: "Apart of the ego too—and Heaven knows how important a part—may be Ucs., undoubtedly is Ucs" (*ibid.*, p. 9). Freud lapses into a very brief literary depression, implicitly wondering if he should scrap his entire theory of the unconscious—"we must admit that the characteristics of being unconscious begins to lose significance" (*ibid.*)—but finishes the chapter with a nod to the future and the hope that somehow this problem can be resolved.

Freud was clear that there were two forms of unconscious: an unconscious *process* and unconscious *content*. Yet, looking back, as no doubt he was in some ways, his prior failure to keep this distinction in mind created a confusion about what he meant when he was referring to *the* unconscious. Was he referring to repressed contents or to the process of repression? But the problem does not stop there. Unconscious processes are not restricted to repressing unwanted ideas. As Freud repeatedly pointed out, there are non-repressed unconscious contents, and so, by implication, there are unconscious processes that do not operate to repress contents but to form contents for other reasons.

Unfortunately, psychoanalysts have tended to focus on the repressed unconscious to the exclusion of the non-repressed unconscious. For decades the non-repressed unconscious has been mischaracterized as simply the "descriptive unconscious", which means that it is not dynamically organized and just rather inert. It could be argued that unconscious memories, for example, are simply part of this descriptive, non-repressed unconscious.

For classical psychoanalysts, the dynamic unconscious refers to the repression of sexual and aggressive drives that seek return to acceptable consciousness in some form or another. *This* unconscious is, by definition, drive-like; it is a pulsion seeking discharge any way it can and when it ropes in thinking it does so rather expeditiously.

Contrast this with Freud's dream work model.

Here the unconscious is an intelligence of form. Its proprioceptive capabilities receive endopsychic data from the storehouse of the unconscious; it also registers "psychically valuable" experiences of the day, sorting them as the day goes on into a kind of pre-dream anteroom, and then it organizes thousands of thoughts, arriving through the intermediate space of lived experience, to be dreamed. The creation of the dream is not only a remarkable aesthetic accomplishment, it is the most sophisticated form of thinking we have. A dream can think hundreds of thoughts in a few seconds, its sheer efficiency breathtaking. It can think past, present, and imagined future in one single image and it can assemble the total range of implicit affects within the day experience, including all ramifying lines of thought that derive from these experiences. With the arrival of the Freudian Pair (see Bollas, 2002) the dream work at last has a companion in the analyst's receptive unconscious and we can see, in the remarkable chains of ideas released through the *process* of free association, infinite lines of meaning. The process of free association is an accomplishment of the ego's work.

It is astonishing, given Freud's emphasis on the dream work (followed by his book on jokes and his book on the psychopathology of everyday life), that he never constructed an explicit theory of unconscious perception. Nor did he spend time indicating how the ego was the vehicle of unconscious organization and communication with the other. I have speculated that Freud, ironically enough, repressed his theory of the unconscious ego. Perhaps he preferred to focus on the repressed unconscious because this seduced the name of the father, the authority *banishing* unwanted ideas. But the ego (the *process* of our mind) is partly formed during the self's relation to the mother within what I have termed the maternal order. The mother *welcomes* the infant into mental life. Banishment of the forbidden is a long way off. Indeed, *this uncon - scious process* is a long period of fulfilling needs and wishes. When Freud repressed knowledge of the maternal order he also rid himself of a theory of mind that was based not on banishment, but on seduction. He "forgot" that part of our unconscious that creatively fulfils our desires all the time, in daydreams, conversations, relations, creative activities, and whatnot.

In his 1915 essay on the unconscious, however, Freud stuns the reader by stating that it is a remarkable thing that the unconscious of one person can react upon the unconscious of the other without going through consciousness. What is remarkable is that he should throw this observation into his metapsychological essay on the unconscious where there is no conceptual room for this thought. What an arresting return of the repressed!

Had Freud unequivocally stated that the ego was not only mostly unconscious but it also created the dream, the symptom, and all works of creativity, then he would have allowed subsequent generations of analysts to see matters differently. His concept of unconscious communication, de-repressed in the above comment about one person's unconscious reacting upon another, *alluded* to unconscious thinking as a highly sophisticated form of thought.

Instead of recognizing that sophistication, Freud "dumbed down" his theory of the unconscious in the structural model. He tried to transpose his topographic model of the mind into the structural model. Thus, the unconscious of the topographic model morphed into the Id. The unconscious of the topographic model and the Id are *not* the same. What we have is a kind of model molestation as Freud tried to segue one theory of the unconscious into the other. It not only sustained a muddle, it contributed to it. More to the point, by morphing the non-repressed unconscious into the *Id* the unconscious was now an "aboriginal" part of the mind that the ego was meant to somehow tame.

It is not difficult to understand what Freud was trying to work out. On the one hand, he knew that part of a person's unconscious life was primitive. It carried the history of the early species within it, it contained infantile sexual phantasies, and it was also the source of the drives. On the other hand, the work of the dream revealed a highly sophisticated form of thinking. How can one reconcile the primitive unconscious with the sophisticated unconscious? In fact, there is no contradiction if one simply understands that *in the beginning* both the form and the contents—that is the process and its productions—of the infant's unconscious were primitive. During the course of time, however, the self's ego becomes more sophisticated. This does not mean that primitive elements of the unconscious—the drives, infantile fantasies, envy, greed, etc.—cease to exist; it simply means that the unconscious processing of these contents becomes more and more sophisticated. Indeed, right from the beginning of life the self is dream working the primitive, transforming urges into images.

Classical analysts to this day think of free association as returning drive derivatives. They rightly point to Freud's writing to support this view. I do not disagree with this, and certainly it is confirmed in clinical practice. However, the *other* unconscious, the non-repressed unconscious, is of little use to classical analysts.

Contrary to the view that this receptive unconscious is the descriptive unconscious, as opposed to the dynamic, the way we organize what impresses us during the day (what is evoked, and what forms we choose to further think them: dreaming, talking, writing, painting, composing, etc.) is actually a highly dynamic process.

Here, I am condensing two points into one, as I would like them to converge for a while before going separate ways. First, we need to be aware of the continued dynamic implications of repression of this kind. Second, Freud's conundrum serves to highlight the hazards of theory formation and both the reach and the limits of theory.

Freud's topographic model is, for example, the best way for us to conceptualize repression. Even if many would throw out his concepts of cathexes and anti-cathexes as outdated, I would submit that we still do not have a better set of metaphors to conceptualize mental intensity. I do not care if Freud's metaphors are hydraulic or electric any more than I care that the Klein–Bion model of ingestion, digestion, and metabolization is alimentary. The point is, does one understand what the metaphor conveys? *This is the definition of metaphor. It is a mental transportation system.* So, does it tell us what it intends to convey or doesn't it?

The topographic model helps us to see how a repressed idea gathers other repressed ideas into mental clusters and how it returns that idea to consciousness. The structural model is less helpful when it comes to conceptualizing repression. But it "sees" the psychodynamics of certain parts of the human mind. It helps us to imagine the play between our drives represented in the concept of the Id and the psychic organization of the rules of our society, allegorized in the theory of our Superego. The agency given the responsibility for sorting out this play, for negotiating, for making compromises, for allowing relief from the needs of the one or the other, is the Ego. This model, now somewhat out of fashion, is invaluable.

The structural model, however, does not advance the topographic model. Although it is historically further along in Freud's thinking and obviously was hugely popular with Freud's daughter and others, it does not address the same issues as the topographic model any more than the topographic model replaces the dream theory model of the unconscious.

Analysts think of newer models of the mind as "advances" in the wrong sort of way. They do increase understanding of the mind but they do *not* replace prior models. This skewed modernist bias, that every intellectual development inevitably improves existent views, has unfortunately resulted in abandonment of important prior models of the mind.

In one psychoanalytical society where I spent a week lecturing and supervising, the analysts were topographical folks and hated the structural model. To put it in geo-political context, the structural model is associated with the Americans and the topographical model with the rest of the classical world. It can actually come down to a kind of culture war. In fact, the structural model and ego psychology were popular first with child analysts, because these models "saw" psycho-development. It was not otherwise visible in the other models of the mind. Try imagining psycho-development according to the topographic model. I wish you luck. The French, in particular, saw the concept of ego development as spurious. They craftily pointed out that as the unconscious was timeless, the entire notion of psycho-development was based on a false psychic premise. Yes, we did obviously develop—there were outward and inward signs of this—but such development had nothing to do *per se* with unconscious life. Unconscious life does not make temporal distinctions of any kind; indeed, it lives in its own a-developmental temporal kingdom. The idea of a psycho-development was a quaint tale told by those who seemed to have a more commercial notion of the self as progressive product. American analysts were the soft target of this critique because not only were they ego psychologists, but also they were selling psychoanalysis to the medical establishment and insurance companies by removing the more radical features of analysis from their representations. No longer could one find in the major texts of the ego psychologists the passage in Freud stressing that the analyst was to catch the drift of the patient's unconscious with his own unconscious. Had they pointed this out to the people of Blue Cross or Blue Shield it would have been a jaw dropping moment.

II

Freud's topographic and structural models come complete with respective images. This helps one to see what they mean. An image, worth a thousand words, serves unconscious purposes. Like a condensed dream fragment it is rather ready-made for the unconscious. It can be more easily internalized and helps a clinician to think about a highly complex matter.

Lacan's Symbolic, Imaginary, and Real does not come as an image, but once we have this tripartite model of meaning in mind it is not difficult to *imagine* the act of listening as involving an interplay between these three orders. Klein's paranoid–schizoid and depressive position theory comes with a small image of arrows (ps-arrow and d-arrow) to signify movement between the two positions. Having internalized this image and the concepts, Kleinians often visualize the material from this perspective.

In addition, all psychoanalysts have unconceptualized theories embedded in the way they practise. Setting aside the inevitability that one's character is a complex set of idiomatic theories functioning on the operational level, clinicians each have individual ways of ordering what they hear and what they say.

It will come as no surprise that each of the differing theories of the psychoanalytical experience constitutes a different perceptual category. If we listen to the material through the structural model, rather than the Kleinian, we will see things differently. Lacan's categories of the Symbolic, Imaginary, and Real gave me a new way of seeing my analysands. Before this I had not seen what I could now see.

This led me to appreciate the value of psychoanalytical theories as *forms* of perception. One theory sees something that other theories do not see. Freud's theory of the logic of sequence imbricated in the flow of any person's free talking allows one to perceive that logic. If we have not learned how to see things in this way then sequential logic will go unnoticed and one will miss an incredibly important field of unconscious material. Klein's ps and d allow one to see forms of splitting and integration that are not otherwise observable.

"A system of thought is something we live in", writes the British philosopher Simon Blackburn (1999) "just as much as a house, and if our intellectual house is cramped and confined, we need to know what better structures are available" (p. 10). Blackburn terms such building "conceptual engineering" (*ibid.*, p. 11) and I think this is a good way to describe the acquisition of psychoanalytical perspectives. As theories are forms of perception, if we settle with just one or two theories we live in a confined intellectual house.

How the psychoanalyst sees human life is obviously conveyed to the patient. The theory by which he thinks constitutes a psychic world-view. Upon entering psychoanalysis the analysand may be unaware of that view, akin to someone getting on an aeroplane headed to a country without knowing where they are going: just a country. There is a difference, however, between landing in Baghdad or Beijing. There is an astonishing difference in the world-views of analysts, just as there are different cities that breed radically different cultures.

Theory, therefore, is not simply a way of perceiving something. It influences the way analysts transform their analysands. Practice follows theory.

Take Freud's theory of free association. If the analyst listens in a state of evenly suspended attentiveness—without trying to concentrate on anything, remember anything, or anticipate anything—his unconscious will occasionally perceive the analysand's unconscious patterns in thought. A form of practice put into place by European analysts, this theory meant waiting, perhaps for long periods of time in sessions, until the analyst got the picture. They suddenly saw a line of thought, which might lead to a comment, or they might elect to remain quiet, meditative.

One person talking; the other listening.

Contrast this with the British School's view of the transference. *All* the people, places, or events in the analysand's narrative are indirect references to the psychoanalyst. If the analyst remains quiet, while the analysand projects a thought into a surrogate, such silence is understood by the analysand—so it is argued—as agreement with the projection. The analyst must therefore translate each and every reference to, or action upon, the self in order to mitigate such a process.

It would be hard to find two more strikingly different ways of perceiving the psychoanalytical experience or two more radically different ways of being with an analysand.

III

There is an ethics of perception. Theories are not simply forms of perception. When practised they *become* ethical decisions.

The Freudian view, just outlined, implicitly assumes the analysand's unconscious construction of meaning. By remaining silent and ostensibly out of the picture, the analyst attends not simply to a line of thought but many divergent lines.

At this moment a thought may arise. "But what about the analyst as a participant? Isn't this a relationship? The idea that the analyst is neutral is a fallacy, as he is affecting his patient all the time."

True, of course.

However, meditation *is* action. It is intended to affect the analysand. It creates the possibility for free speech. By creating the illusion of neutrality the analyst partly suspends the oversight of consciousness. Analysts who *practise* neutrality enable the patient's free associations to guide the sessions. They are more receptive to the analysand's free talking than analysts who believe that analysis is a highly interactive event. Inevitably, highly interactive analysts will interpersonalize a session. The illusion of neutrality is intended to function as much for the analyst as the analysand. The analyst believes he is just listening. This is not dissimilar to a reader who believes he or she is just reading, or a listener who is just listening to music.

Let us ask a different question. How might one's subjective response to the analysand be discoverable? Setting aside the reality that an analyst—like a reader or listener to music—should be so deeply lost in listening that he would not know how to answer this question, let's still proceed. Where *is* his subjective response to be found? *If* we really do believe in the unconscious, then this question has a most disconcerting answer. Neutrality recognizes a plain fact. Even though we have some conscious responses to what our analysands say and do, we rarely know our "personal" unconscious response. Neutralized by our unconscious, we simply do not have access to the sort of information the question seeks. Frustrating as this fact of our life is, if we cheat—and try to manufacture news from our unconscious, if for no other reason than to come up with some kind of story-line—we deny ourselves and our patients *the fact* of living as an unconscious being.

IV

Theories vary in depth and range of view.

A *psychoanalytical theory* only becomes useful when it has entered the psychoanalyst's receptive unconscious. Joining other theories, it will operate according to the dictates of the analytical experience in a session. Sometimes a theory will pop into consciousness not before the clinician has come to its realization, but afterwards. It functions in much of the way "genera" (Bollas, 1992) work, a concept I coined to identify the arrival of new unconscious realizations that lead to a different way of viewing life.

Some will see here what seems to be a reversal of one of Freud's paradigms: the movement of unconscious issues into consciousness. Freud was rightly concentrating on unconscious conflicts and believed that moving them into consciousness was therapeutically efficacious. That is certainly true some of the time, although I have argued that the greater part of psychic change occurs unconsciously and need not enter consciousness, either in the analyst or in the analysand. My reversal of Freud's paradigm accounts for the obvious and ordinary internalizations of informative models that people absorb all the time to become part of their unconscious structure. Were this not so we would neither learn nor benefit from lived experience.

The legitimacy of any one psychoanalytical theory resides in its function as a form of perception. To plumb the depths of this depth psychology a theory must have a *capacity for* unconscious perception. Some theories obviously have greater depth than others. Therein lies a challenge to all psychoanalysts, because the deeper a theory, the harder it is for a psychoanalyst to embrace it. Not only because it takes longer to acquire and structuralize, but because it inevitably involves the clinician in a more exacting personal experience.

Theories, then, have varying degrees of depth potential.

Freud's theory of the dream work gives meaning to the term depth psychology; indeed, he defined depth psychology as the interpretation of dreams. His understanding of how the dream works the previous day's experiences, guided by the self's psychic history, *is* depth psychology. The dream work theory embraces both the phylogentic and the ontological realms of human subjectivity. His use of free association allows us to see some of the work of that depth psychology, thus enabling us to follow chains of ideas that may occur just for a few seconds in a session, or trains of thought that may be elaborated over a life span.

Freud's dream work theory is a complex perceptual matrix that takes years to acquire. Like Lacan's theory of the Symbolic,

Imaginary, and Real, or Klein's infantile mind theory, the analyst learning these models must be patient as the acquisition of a form of perception takes time

V

Most students seek "super-vision" from a clinician steeped in one model of the mind who is gifted in conveying how one can see the material from his or her particular perspective.

An irony of psychoanalytical practice, however, is that for theory to be effective, once it is grasped it must then drop out of consciousness. For this to happen the supervisor must sense when the supervisee has understood the basic paradigms being taught. Once this has happened it is time to stop.

This does not always happen. While it is understandable that a supervisor or teacher will outline, discuss, and indicate how a theory can help the student comprehend certain clinical material it is not so common for the teacher to indicate to the student that after internalization it is in the best interests of the patient and the analyst for the analyst to be without conscious preconception. To this day it is all too widespread a public practice to hear analysts talking about finding the drive derivative in the material, or the ego position, or the here and now transference, or the true self, extending the idea that one can see these matters *continuously* in consciousness.

One of the most troubling features of psychoanalytical training is the degree to which some theories are meant to reside in the analyst's conscious mind all the time. That may be keeping an eye on the analysand's ego position, or projective identifications in the here and now transference, or the drive derivative, or the analyst's personal effect on the analysand. The retention of such theories in consciousness—not allowed to sift down into the unconscious to join other theories—not only leads to a hypertrophied consciousness, but amounts to an unwitting evisceration of the work with unconscious experience. It is unsurprising that a considerable number of analysts are now wondering if the unconscious exists. Little wonder, then, that there is an embarrassing soap opera romancing of consciousness theory in psychoanalysis.

VI

Schools of psychoanalysis are invaluable. It is an ethical obligation, in my view, for all psychoanalysts to immerse themselves in the theoretical orientation of the major schools of psychoanalysis: Freudian, Kleinian, Hartmanian, Kohutian, Bionian, Winnicottian, and Lacanian. To do so is to increase one's perceptual ability, to expand one's mind, to greet patients with a wisdom that can only be realized by passage through difference.

A school usually studies the text of one or two seminal thinkers. Students are taught by experts in that school, sometimes by the seminal thinker, and later by those who have carefully read and scrutinized the writing. Great teachers are invaluable because the way they teach sinks down into the unconscious life of a student and is effective for a lifetime.

A theory is a metasensual phenomenon. It allows one to see something not seen by other theories; to have as an unconscious possibility should clinical need for it arise. To declare oneself against other schools of thought is like someone stating that one is an eye person and does not like the ear or auditory sense data, or for someone to declare that they trust what they hear, but never trust what they smell. The metasensual equivalent, operating in psychoanalysis today—where one needs all the differing perspectives one can possibly structuralize in the course of time—is a form of auto-castration. To entirely oppose the Kleinian or Lacanian view of mental life is to wilfully reduce one's psychic capability as an analyst.

Psychoanalysts need to learn all the theories they can so that they may become unconscious perception-structures enabling practitioners to participate more deeply in the psychoanalytical experience. The analysand's unconscious will sense the range of perceptive receptiveness of the psychoanalyst. This will both deepen and broaden the analysand's skill in unconscious communication. While the work of rendering symptoms, character distortions, pathologic structures, and trauma into consciousness remains a crucial feature of a psychoanalysis, *the work of the uncon - scious* will increase the analysand's capacity for unconscious perception, creativity, and communication. We see this not so much in the removal of a symptom, pathologic structure, or character deformation (although those, too, will go or be modified) we see it in the way the analysand engages life in a more creative way.

If theory is perception, if it indicates an ethics of practice, it also serves as a sign of the limits of consciousness. However much a theory presumes to tell us something about a person, its actual function is less in what it discovers than in how it sees. Klein's theory of what takes place in the first year of life is less significant than the allegoric perceptual structure that permits us to imagine infancy. Lacan's theory of the subject's instantiation through the chain of signifiers is less a theory of found unconscious meanings than a portal to entering a world of linguistic relations.

Even though the psychoanalyst can only ever know unconscious expression through its effects (or derivatives), these complex articulations are the matrix of our being. As psychoanalytic theories are, among other things, forms of perception, each will inevitably be of some use in helping us to unconsciously perceive unconscious processes and their contents.

CHAPTER FIVE

On transference interpretation as a resistance to free association

One of Freud's first understandings of transference was the transportation of unconscious mental contents to consciousness. In *The Interpretation of Dreams* he wrote:

> We learn . . . that an unconscious idea is as such quite incapable of entering the preconscious and that it can only exercise any effect thereby establishing a connection with an idea which already belongs to the preconscious, by transferring its intensity on to it and by getting itself 'covered' by it. Here we have the fact of 'transference', which provides an explanation of so many striking phenomena in the mental life of neurotics. The preconscious idea, which thus acquires an undeserved degree of intensity, may either be left unaltered by the transference, or it may have a modification forced upon it, derived from the content of the idea which effects the transference. [Freud, 1900a, pp. 562–563]

In this essay I focus on the ways in which this view of transference was to become demoted and limited to a more specific understanding of what takes place in the Transference (denoted here by a capital letter). I argue that modern psychoanalysis should return to Freud's early view in order to rediscover its wisdom.

Freud provided a model of analytical technique that depended entirely on *the above kind of transfer*. I have termed this model the Freudian Pair (Bollas, 2002, p. 7), the free associating analysand and the evenly suspended analyst, a relation specifically designed to elicit unconscious lines of thought with the aim of discovering some of the latent mental contents. This radical view of Freud's theory has been systematically marginalized by future generations of psychoanalysts, and it is worth once again bringing it into our minds. The following two passages are from Freud's "Two ency-clopaedia articles" written in 1922.

The first passage describes the position and the function of the analysand:

> The treatment is begun by the patient being required to put himself in the position of an attentive and dispassionate self-observer, merely to read off all the time the surface of his consciousness, and on the one hand to make a duty of the most complete honesty while on the other hand not to hold back any idea from communication even if (1) he feels that it is too disagreeable or if (2) he judges that it is nonsensical or (3) too unimportant or (4) irrelevant to what is being looked for. It is uniformly found that precisely those ideas which provoke these last-mentioned reactions are of particular value in discovering the fogotten material [Freud, 1923a, p. 238].

More could be said about this. But here we can note that the idea that the analysand's dark secrets are of high value is dismissed by Freud. Deep in the heart of the everyday, Freud places the highest value on what would appear to be irrelevant. Note how he defines the position and function of the analyst who is listening to the free associating patient:

> Experience soon showed that the attitude which the analytic physi-cian could most advantageously adopt was to surrender himself to his own unconscious mental activity, in a state of evenly suspended attention, to avoid so far as possible reflection and the construction of conscious expectations, not to try to fix anything he heard partic-ularly in his memory, and by these means to catch the drift of the patient's unconscious with his own unconscious. [*ibid.*, p. 239]

Much can be said about this remarkable passage, but I emphasize only one element because *it is this element* that most schools of psychoanalysis consistently refuse to recognize, much less teach. Freud is unequivocal in stating that the work of a psychoanalysis is *unconscious to unconscious*. It is the accomplishment of this remarkable "object relation" that gives rise to my term the Freudian Pair, because I believe we must keep this in mind in our work at all times.

Listening in this manner leads on occasion to a type of revelation. The psychoanalyst (or it could be the analysand), heretofore lost in thought, is struck by the logic of the sequence of ideas presented by the unconscious. First, latent mental contents are received by the psychoanalyst's unconscious, which perceives this logic, and then his or her consciousness is struck by the ideas thus far hidden from conscious awareness.

In addition to accomplishing a transfer from unconscious thinking to conscious thought, we know that the Freudian Pair also functions as an unconscious thinking unit. ("Two heads are better than one.")

Only a fraction of what the analysand is thinking can strike the analyst; evocative material is usually part of a sustained series of unconscious questions on the part of the analysand. His unconscious recognizes the analyst as a mental function constituted through a relationship. The analysand understands that, as the psychoanalyst is receptive to free association, unconscious thinking can take place between two minds that have divided functions: the one mind to speak openly without reflection or censorship and the other mind to listen freely.

It is almost a cliché to say that the transference is ubiquitous, that it is everywhere. However, the *technique* of transference, invented by and for psychoanalysis via the process of free association, is not ubiquitous but unique to the analytical situation.

The elision of these two forms of transference serves as the foundation of a certain type of irony in contemporary analytical discourse. Psychoanalysts who work within the Freudian Pair are often asked "What about the Transference?" In a moment I shall come to the forms of transference to which this question is ordinarily directed, but it is important to see that it is this very question that eliminates the transference unique to psychoanalysis.

The above question oblates a far more important issue: "Does the analyst understand the analysand's transference?" This queries whether the psychoanalyst understands the need of the analysand to think freely in the presence of the psychoanalyst, who is also meant to listen *with an open mind*. It asks whether or not there has been a successful division of mental function (The Freudian Pair) as part of the psychoanalytical process.

In *this context*, this question does not ask to which figure in the analysand's history the patient is speaking. Neither does it wonder what internal object is being represented by the analysand through a specific mental object within the field of free association.

There is no psychoanalyst who does not know the story of Freud's discovery of the Transference. Perhaps most famously addressed in his regrets about Dora, Freud argued that the analysis broke down because he failed to recognize the young woman's Transference to him. From this momentous revelation many of the subsequent analytical understandings of the Transference emerged. The Transference refers to unconscious wishes or relived memories of former relations to earlier objects in the patient's life that are projected into or on to the analyst and that have, among other things, the effect of disturbing the Freudian Pair.

Yet, what about the other transference? The transference that all along has been operating in the Freudian Pair, the transference that Freud recognized as "unobjectionable"? (1912b, p. 105). As discussed, this transference involves the deployment of mental functions that facilitate the possibility of unconscious thinking, unconscious creativity, and unconscious communication between the two participants. Could this transfer of mental function become at times so impeded by the Transference that it might be suspended until it is worked through? Surely this might be so. A patient might, for example, be so intimidated by some aspect of his imagined relationship to the analyst that he decides to remain silent and thus opt out of that division of mental function that is crucial to the Freudian Pair.

There is, however, no intrinsic evidence provided by Freud from his work with Dora that the Transference interfered with her transfer of unconscious ideas through the Freudian Pair. Indeed, the question "Does the Transference interfere with the Freudian transference?" is one that seems to have slipped our minds. There seems to have been an automatic assumption that if the analysand is engaged in the Transference, then the Freudian transference ceases to exist.

The focus on free association in the psychoanalytical process may become suspended. According to the analytical literature, this shift is the fault of the patient who, by virtue of wish, memory, or object relation, interferes with the analytical process. Not, incidentally, a view that Freud supported. What is not recognized is that the suspension of the division of mental function central to the Freudian Pair is derived from the psychoanalyst's preoccupation with the Transference. From Dora onwards the analytical literature reveals an increasing preoccupation with the Transference and correspondingly there is a dramatic decrease, not only in the literature on free association but, more tellingly, in the intellectual exploration of this division of function.

It is not the analysand's insistence upon the movement of the Transference that has marginalized the true Freudian transference. It is the psychoanalyst who has been dislodged by the ubiquitous Transference that takes place in all object relations.

In so far as the Freudian transference refers to the division of mental function, it is a process that is not influenced by its own contents. Whatever wish, memory, or internal relation the patient may project on to the analyst—that is whatever content it reveals—does not shut down the mind that thinks it. When Bion referred to the task of the analyst, saying that he or she should be "without memory or desire", he is really doing nothing more nor less than pointing out that every psychoanalyst should *be* a psychoanalyst when seeing a patient. That is, every analyst should engage in a division of mental function that constitutes the Freudian Pair.

But is the Transference bound to interfere with the Freudian Pair? If the analysand unconsciously projects a critical father into the analyst will this not inevitably influence that freedom of thought assumed to be taking place in the process? For example, will this lead the analysand to suspend communications that will in turn earn the disapproval of the analyst?

This may occur if the patient has a thought that crosses the mind, which he or she finds difficult to report precisely because it might earn disapproval. Such occasions are often announced through a type of silence or evasive speech that, despite the patient's intentions, will flag up resistance and usually lead either the patient or the psychoanalyst to interpret it. So it is that overt resistance, such as silence, achieves the paradoxical result of drawing attention to unwanted mental contents.

Freud believed that the thought which the patient viewed as the most important—in the above example, the secret that cannot be disclosed—was not, in fact, the most significant but, to the contrary, the least important. He made it clear that the most important free associations were the apparently irrelevant ideas; the seemingly least significant being of the highest value. The question is, what difference does it make to the Freudian Pair if the analysand censors a certain mental content but none the less proceeds to talk about other things on his mind? Let us assume for the moment that fear of the analyst's disapproval convinces the patient to avoid talking about something. Does that disable the process of free association?

In short, the answer is that it does not. The patient might think that by not reporting a troubling idea he or she was not talking about what was really on the mind. However, that will only be true of the manifest content. The patient may not have been talking about what was consciously in mind but, as we know, the Freudian definition of what is on the self's mind is determined by the complexity of the unconscious—by all the interests occurring at any moment in psychic time driven by unconscious desires, memories, anxieties, curiosities, and so forth.

It may be asked, what about unconscious resistances based upon unconscious Transferences? Is it not true that such structures will interfere with, or significantly distort, the free associative process in such a way that until that distortion is interpreted the lines of thought revealed would be under the influence of Transference resistance? This is surely a more credible thesis, but, none the less, one that misses the point. Free association reveals lines of thought only as long as the analysand keeps thinking associatively. As long as the analysand moves from one topic to another he or she will continue to think unconsciously out loud. Such thought processes are of course highly condensed and full of overdeterminants, so that from phrase to phrase (I use the musical metaphor to describe a unit of free associative logic) many ideas are being thought. A particular mental content could undergo distortion due to self censorship, but, as I have said, such distortions actually draw attention to the content and bring it into the foreground. More to the point, it is an absurdity to think that the plenitude of ideas moving along in psychic time could in themselves be resisted successfully.

Unconscious thinking is not held in any single mental idea, but takes place as a logical process. It is revealed not in one narrative unit—a patient talking about baking cakes, for example —but in the links between narrative units. In the caesura one finds the logical possibilities. It is exactly in and through these gaps that the logic of thought occurs which is never subordinate to the Transference.

But is it not true that all association is part of a conscious or unconscious rhetorical strategy? As one speaks, to follow Heimann and others, is it not right to ask who is speaking, to whom, about what, and why now? Is it not also true that all speech is a form of action, an "illocutionary act", as Austin put it, or a "speech act", according to Searle, that always involves a Transference directed at an object? These are questions posed from the perspectives of object relations theory.

One of the most interesting aspects of looking at detailed clinical material is to discover Transference intentions and yet to find at the same time that *other lines of unconscious thought* continue none the less. How are we to understand this? How can unconscious phrases be part of a rhetorical strategy—indeed, be the voice of some part of a self speaking to some object—and yet still remain *outside* or *alongside* this intent?

A patient may say "I remember only yesterday baking a cake". Saying this may be part of a mood of self idealization, and, in speaking this thought to the analyst, the aim may be to elicit the analyst's love of the patient as a worthy soul who is doing something good. The psychoanalyst may feel the intent of this romantic communication. But the content is not yet part of a chain of ideas; it is not yet, in other words, either a free association or an expression of unconscious logic. It remains to be seen what the patient says next. But let us assume that the patient remains in a self idealizing mood and mentions next a friend who ruined a dessert, then talks about reading a book about overly needy children and how to work with them, then talks about the self's own distance from an intrusive mother; then talks about . . . Now, for a while we can see the intent in the rhetorical strategy: the patient seeks to gain the analyst's romantic sympathies by presenting the self as ideal. But as the patient talks on and on, moving from one topic to another, the rhetorical strategy begins to break down under the disseminative effect of the movement of ideas that cannot be simplified into any Transference scheme.

In other words, after a while, the object relational structure implicit in the illocutionary act is superseded by the flow of ideas. Even if the object relation—seeking the approval of the analyst—is sustained as a mood in the analysand, or is consciously comprehended by both as an all too familiar strategy, the mere act of *speaking on*, of proceeding according to the unconscious dictat of free association, will break the success of the strategy.

It is not only interpretation that can dissolve the Transference. The mere passage of time drives the process of free association that inevitably leads to *other* thoughts.

Of course, we see this all the time in the ordinary scenes of life. We see how a person begins to tell a story with the intent of gaining favour. We may observe the positive disposition of the listener, only to see over time that what the speaker actually says does not ultimately fulfil this original intent but eventually confuses or annoys the audience. In other words, we know all too well that if we speak on and on, whatever the illocutionary intent, whatever the fantasy guiding utterance, the unconscious logic of the self's discourse speaks for itself. In this respect it is not part of the Transference—indeed, very often it unconsciously belies it.

If we know this from ordinary life experience, why has our theory of Transference occluded our view of free association? Why have we made such a fundamental mistake in our own thinking?

We have gained the best of our insights from Freud's own transforming visions, but I think we have probably inherited his worst traits as well, and they can stay with us far too long. Freud's error was to assume that his failure to understand and to interpret the Transference to Dora (and to subsequent patients) was responsible for the failure of that analysis. By extension, psychoanalysts have assumed that the mutative effect of psychoanalysis can only take place through analysis of Transference.

In fact, in a footnote to his Postscript about Dora, Freud dismissed the idea that failure to interpret the Transference was responsible for the premature ending of this analysis.

> The longer the interval of time that separates me from the end of this analysis, the more probable it seems to me that the fault in my

technique lay in this omission: I failed to discover in time and to inform the patient that her homosexual (gynaecophilic) love for Frau K. was the strongest unconscious current in her mental life. [Freud, 1905e, p. 120]

So . . . out with the Transference and in with the failure of correct understanding. Or perhaps it is more complex than this. Freud refers to the "interval of time" that is essential to the process of free association, and it is this passing of time that yields for him the missing interpretation. Is it really true that this interpretation would have changed the course of the analysis? Who knows? I rather doubt it. What Freud unconsciously re-asserts is the need for time to pass and for the chain of ideas to march on, and in so doing he acknowledges the actual failure. To his unconscious credit, he throws out the theory that his failure to comprehend the Transference was the heart of the matter. His footnote recognized the importance of the passage of time and the introduction of new ideas. What he, and many others since, did not recognize was that this footnote constituted a subtle critique of the theory of Transference as the heart of the analytical enterprise.

Let us think about Freud's theory of the Transference as the missing link. Let us assume for a moment that it was indeed his failure to understand Dora's Transference that was responsible for the failure of that analysis. Let us assume that Freud had understood the Transference and had interpreted it. Do we agree, then, that the analysis would have been a success? Well, some would immediately object that Freud's failure to understand his own countertransference was responsible for this failure. So let us assume for discussion's sake that Freud understood and utilized through apt interpretation both the Transference and the countertransference. Let us go to an extreme and further imagine that he understood the underlying wishes, memories, and internal object structures that were expressed by Dora as illocutionary actions. Would that interpretation have been the mutative factor?

Before I address this directly I want to point out a flaw in this thinking. It assumes that what has been missing or left out in the function, understanding, or narrative of a situation is responsible for the failure of the situation to thrive. The *crie de coeur* of the moment—"What about the Transference?"—stands, then, for the logic that the omitted must be the cause of failure. If only "it" had been included things would have been different.

I am not at all sure that, even had Freud understood both Dora's Transference and his own countertransference, the analysis would have been a success. In any analysand's termination of an analysis it is highly unlikely that either participant will actually know why "it" ended. There are as many possible explanations for an ending as there are for a beginning, as there are for an interruption, as there are indeed for any human phenomenon.

"What about the Transference?" has become in psychoanalysis a signifier for "What about the omitted?" It concretizes this unconscious issue by presuming there is always one answer to the question "Why has this failed?", and it refuses the possibility that analysts will ever know why some patients leave analysis or why some analyses do not thrive.

In an increasingly wide arc of the present psychoanalytical world it is assumed that if an analysis has not gone well then somehow the psychoanalyst failed to understand and interpret the Transference. Transference *here*, however, as the name for the missing, constitutes a refusal to accept the existence of the uncertain, of the unknowable. To know and to interpret the Transference is to solve any problem posed by the analysand, and certainly it is this concept to which the analytical group turns when troubled by a case presentation that is not so easily understood.

The interesting result of this line of thinking is that the Transference becomes *the solution* to the question of the analysand's unconscious. "What about the Transference?" leads many in the analytical world to quickly address this issue and assume that in so doing they are more in touch with the course of the analysis. By interpreting the Transference, the analyst believes he is more able to reach the patient, less likely to be in the dark, floundering around as a mere conscious being in the infinitely subtle subtexts generated by unconscious lines of thought.

When discussing a case presentation, psychoanalysts not caught up in the here and now Transference interpretation will "pick up" on many different dimensions. As any analysis is full of unconscious lines of thought and movements, it is not surprising that any group of free thinking analysts will diverge in their views of what they find significant. Even the analyst is likely to have different thoughts and feelings about the material when presenting a patient to colleagues than when he or she was in the session. If the group studies a session over a long period of time, further lines of thought emerge into consciousness. It is a common feature of applied psychoanalysis in literary criticism that readers discover that returning again and again to the same text yields new insights into what appear to be latent contents. In other words, most communications, whether by a patient speaking to the analyst or a poet writing a poem, are highly overdetermined and will yield multiple meanings over time. This should not be surprising to psychoanalysts who presume to be the intellectual custodians of the study of unconscious processes of thought.

II

Let us now turn to the current preoccupation—one might say obsession—with the requirement that the analyst interpret the here and now Transference. This perspective assumes that the people, places, and events narrated by the analysand always partly refer to the psychoanalyst. In addition, it is assumed that the analysand's narrative is an unconscious illocutionary act directed towards the analyst.

This way of listening to the material has bowdlerized and canalized the rich tradition of listening offered by Freud's view of free association. It has resulted in a profound shift in psychoanalysis, often in the name of the "British School". Its insistent question, "What about the here and now Transference?", demands of the clinician that he or she *hear the material in terms of the presumed uncon - scious references to the psychoanalyst.*

Outside the British School, many have a very different way of responding to the Transference: that one thinks about the transference *when it comes to mind.* We should call this latter group the "now and then" transference interpreters. "Now and then" interpreters are as schooled as "here and now" interpreters in the understanding of the Transference, but they think about the material as a reference to the clinician only when such a thought enters the analyst's consciousness spontaneously and without prejudice.

Here and now interpreters, on the other hand, are highly prejudiced. For them it is axiomatic that the analysand's narrative *always* refers to the psychoanalyst, and for some it constitutes an action in the Transference. Before a session begins the psychoanalyst knows that he or she will listen to the people, places, and events described as portrayals of the analysand's experience of the psychoanalyst in the here and now. The task of the analyst is to interpret this to the analysand, sooner rather than later, as delay would appear to the analysand as an act of complicity: i.e., the analyst is too afraid to interpret, too depressed to say anything, perhaps too excited to interpret and hoping for more of the same, and so on and so forth.

There are many worrying features of this prejudice, above all, perhaps, the fact that this way of listening constitutes an idea of reference. All psychoanalysts are certainly aware, in theory, that anyone can construct a listening system based on a selective fact.

It is disturbing that this paranoid listening system has led the analyst to view the analysand as always trying to get something over on him, even when the analysand is being cooperative. In the extreme—but not uncommonly—analysts who have adopted this practice become worryingly authoritarian, pronouncing the real hidden meanings to the analysand who, if he or she resists such imposed truths, is then caught up in a vicious circle of being subjected to accusations that he or she is attempting to destroy the analysis.

How and in what ways has this prejudice affected the Freudian Pair? First, the analysand will unconsciously perceive that the psychoanalyst is not listening with an open mind. The predictable and redundant nature of this form of listening nullifies the wish to communicate. It announces a lack of capacity in the psychoanalyst to *be unconscious* and thus able to receive the other's unconscious communications.

Second, the analysand gradually understands that the analyst seeks meaning around the analysand's presumed relation to the psychoanalyst: i.e., there is something that assumes priority in the hierarchy of meaning. Recall for a moment Freud's wisdom in his definition of the way the psychoanalyst listens: that it is the least relevant idea which he believes carries the most significant meaning. Here and now interpreters so privilege the Transference communication that all other unconscious meanings resident in the patient's communications are eliminated.

Third, when the psychoanalyst interprets immediately in the Transference, he or she is foreclosing the flow of thought essential to the free associative process. No chain of meaning can be established, as this is denied in the first place by the analyst's persistent interpretation. Psychoanalysts trained in this tradition genuinely and sincerely do not believe in free association. They have had no experience of it from their analysands because they have adopted a technique that systematically refuses it. Their analyses become, then, self-fulfilling prophecies. Armed with the view that the analysand's communications must be hidden references to the analyst's self, they repeatedly make such links. The potentially alienating effect this has on the patient will, not surprisingly, frequently evoke a negative transference, thus condemning the analysis to become a realisation of what André Green terms the "work of the negative".

It is interesting that psychoanalysts who discuss their cases individually have a much better opportunity to regain contact with their Freudian heritage, or, if they have not been schooled in this approach, to learn how to do it. Analysts in groups are a different matter. Almost invariably when discussing a presentation, one or other member of a group will say "But what about the Transference?", and presto, the group's thought processes evaporate, their ability to muse on the material in that state of reverie of which Bion writes with such eloquence is foreclosed. This interruption of free thought by the Transference is so damaging that the group cannot recover its analytical mind.

In other words, ironically enough, one can see *in the here and now* how this form of thinking destroys a group's reverie: how the imperious here and now Transference interpretation interrupts psychoanalytical musing.

III

Psychoanalysis is a solitary enterprise and, even though unconscious life is non-material and hidden in the mists of the descriptive unconscious, psychoanalysts decided at some point in time to present their work to one another in the infamous case conference. Where once there had been only one analytical mind present to listen to the patient, now there could be four, five, or eight. Psychoanalytical practice, therefore, became partly determined by the view of the group. It was this development more than any other that was responsible, in my view, for the birth, growth, and dissemination of a delusion. "What about the Transference?" became so predictable a question for anyone presenting to others, whether in a training situation or to groups of colleagues, that presenters knew it would be coming, and in time the analysts started making these interpretations just so that they could defend their work in the midst of the group.

I mean, who wanted to appear stupid? And that is how it appeared in the British School if, when asked about what was happening in the Transference, the psychoanalyst did not have an answer. Where in the session had the analyst demonstrated that he or she knew about the here and now Transference? Where in the session had the analyst actually interpreted in the Transference? There became only one way to establish one's analytical credibility in such an environment and that was to join in with the movement and demonstrate before one's colleagues that one could do this as well as the rest.

Here psychoanalysts in groups were doing to each other what they were doing to their patients. Presenting analysts knew their colleagues would not listen to the session with an open mind, but would automatically focus on the Transference. Although other themes might be considered from time to time and other issues mentioned, the crux of the presentation lay in how the analysand was talking about the analyst in the material, and in what the analysand was doing to the analyst through such talk. Before long, practising clinicians were no longer bringing material that was "open", but were bringing sessions meant to demonstrate their participation in their group's way of thinking. This thinking was closed-minded and so had the sessions demonstrated closed-mindedness.

Delusional thinking thrives in persecutory environments and spreads with great success in and through groups. The solitary deluded patient in a hospital who thinks that the radio disc jockey is talking to him will not fare so well unless five or six other patients begin to have the same idea and then the idea spreads and can be difficult to contain. If ten or twenty people share the delusion, then the beginnings of a system of delusional belief is established that can last for thousands of years.

One of the functions of delusional thinking is to simplify complexity. Being a psychoanalyst is certainly to occupy a place perhaps more complex than any other human relation. To Freud's lasting credit, he never organized his many views of mental life and human relations into a single system of thought. He knew, and he conveyed the fact, that his subject was simply too overdetermined for such systematic organization.

Why would so many psychoanalysts opt for an extreme form of Transference interpretation in which mental life was reduced to simple terms of reference? It is not difficult to see that one reason would be that this rescues the psychoanalyst from the burden of engaging in a relationship too far from consciousness.

In the British School, "What about the Transference?" became a speech act: "stop thinking about anything else!" It sought to resolve an anxiety: "How can I feel effective in a place like this?"

It did so by not thinking. A mantra—"what about the Transference—occupied these analysts' minds and rid them of any meaningful contact with the density of the analysand's unconscious life.

IV

The question of Dora signifies the impossible task that faces the psychoanalyst who believes that he or she should know what is taking place in the here and now of unconscious communications. The view that Freud had not understood the Transference, or later the countertransference, leads to the notion that, by comprehending the Transference and the countertransference, psychoanalysts were understanding their patients. These terms became overloaded with meaning for psychoanalysts. Announcing that one was addressing the Transference and the countertransference became *signs* that one had understood the unconscious.

I have marginalized the Transference in order to make a single point. The many and diverse understandings of the types of Transference in an analysis remains an important *part* of the total picture of what takes place in any psychoanalysis. It is more than ironic that the here and now transference zealots have also denuded the Transference of its variegated and diverse complexities.

It would be an error to regard the views put forward in this essay as a dismissal of the important communicative value of the many types of Transference. My aim has been limited. First, I have sought to indicate how and why over-emphasis of the here and now transference interpretation has become a resistance to the transference as first envisioned by Freud. Second, I have raised a type of alarm, pointing to an illness now within psychoanalysis itself, a form of paranoia perpetuated by a group-delusional process that has transformed a selected fact into a total truth.

REFERENCES

Austin, J. L. (1962). *How To Do Things With Words*. Oxford: Oxford University Press.

Blackburn, S. (1999). *Think: A Compelling Introduction to Philosophy*. Oxford: Oxford University Press.

Bollas, C. (1987). *The Shadow of the Object*. London: Free Association.

Bollas, C. (1989). *Forces of Destiny*. London: Free Association.

Bollas, C. (1992). *Being a Character*. London: Routledge.

Bollas, C. (1992). The fascist state of mind. In: *Being a Character* (pp. 193–217). London, Routledge.

Bollas, C. (1995). *Cracking Up*. London: Routledge.

Bollas, C. (1999). *The Mystery of Things*. London: Routledge.

Bollas, C. (2002). *Free Association*. London: Icon.

Brenner, C. (1982). *The Mind in Conflict*. New York: International Universities Press.

Eigen, M. (2004). *The Electrified Tightrope*. London: Karnac.

Freud, S. (1895d). *Studies on Hysteria*. *S.E.*, 11. London: Hogarth.

Freud, S. (1900a). *The Interpretation of Dreams*. *S.E.*, 4–5. London: Hogarth.

Freud, S. (1905e). Fragment of an analysis of a case of hysteria. *S.E.*, 7. London: Hogarth.

Freud, S. (1909d). *Notes Upon a Case of Obsessional Neurosis. S.E., 10*: 152–257. London: Hogarth.

Freud, S. (1912e). Recommendations to physicians practising psycho-analysis. *S.E., 12*. London: Hogarth.

Freud, S. (1913c). On beginning the treatment. *S.E., 12*. London: Hogarth.

Freud, S. (1915e). The unconscious. *S.E., 14*. London: Hogarth.

Freud, S. (1923a) Two encyclopaedia articles. *S.E., 18*. London: Hogarth.

Freud, S. (1923b). *The Ego and the Id. S.E., 19*. London: Hogarth.

Freud, S. (1933a). *New Introductory Lectures. S.E., 22*. London: Hogarth.

Freud, S. (1912b). The dynamics of transference. *S.E., 12*. London: Hogarth.

Phillips, A. (2002). *Equals*. London: Faber & Faber.

Pontalis, J.-B. (1981). *Frontiers in Psychoanalysis*. London: Hogarth.

Ryle, G. (1949). *The Concept of Mind*. Chicago, Ill: University of Chicago Press.

Schachtel, E. G. (1984). *Metamorphosis: on the Development of Affect, Perception, Attention, and Memory*. New York: Da Capo Press.